Soul–
Healing
Love

Ten Practical,
Easy-to-Learn Techniques
for Couples in Crisis

Beverly and Tom Rodgers

Resource Publications, Inc.
San Jose, California

Reprint Department
Resource Publications, Inc.
160 E. Virginia Street #290
San Jose, CA 95112-5876
(408) 286-8505 (voice)
(408) 287-8748 (fax)

Library of Congress Cataloging-in-Publication Data

Rodgers, Beverly, 1954–
    Soul-healing love: ten practical, easy-to-learn techniques for couples in crisis / Beverly and Tom Rodgers.
        p.   cm.
    Includes bibliographical references.
    ISBN 0-89390-434-1 (pbk.)
    1. Marriage—Religious aspects—Christianity.   2. Love—Religious aspects—Christianity.   3. Spouses—Religious life.   I. Rodgers, Thomas A., 1950–   .   II. Title.
    BV4596.M3R64   1998
    248.8'44—dc21   98-15104

Printed in the United States of America.
    00 01 02 | 5 4 3 2

Editorial director: Nick Wagner
Project manager: Mike Sagara
Copyeditor: Robin Witkin

Contents

List of Exercises

Exercise 8: The Behavior Change Request

Teaches you how to ask your partner to change unwanted behavior, without conflict.

Exercise 9: Mirroring or Parroting

A listening technique that helps you hear and be heard without misunderstanding and misinterpretation.

Exercise 10: The Giving of Presents

A list of the things that your spouse can do that make you feel warm, secure, and cared for.

Foreword

Marriages in this country are crumbling. Statistically speaking, half of them will end in divorce. Couples are looking for a way out of their struggles. As for much of the healing that occurs, the journey is a spiritual one. *Soul-Healing Love* provides a road map for couples to follow on their spiritual journey. It gives practical guidance for transforming struggles into sacredness and fear into faith.

It is written from the heart of a couple who not only talks the real talk, but walks the real walk. Bev and Tom Rodgers have earned the right to lead others in the journey of relationship.

This book should he on the nightstand of every couple who wishes to heal or enrich their relationship. It gives you answers you seek and solutions you need to create a loving marriage.

Patricia Love, EdD
Director of Austin Family Institute
Author of *Hot Monogamy*

Introduction

Romantic love is still the mystical, sought-after prize it has been for centuries. Even with countless manuscripts written and copious theories on the subject expounded, love's mysteries still elude many of us.

Love has been depicted as practical, biblical, mystical, conscious, unconscious, rational, irrational, logical, illogical, and just plain unexplainable. Amidst all of this, our society continues to be fascinated with it. Tom and I have been Christian marriage counselors for the past eighteen years. We have treated all types of couples from all walks of life. After watching their struggles and feeling their pain, we believe that love is all of the above and more. Discovering more about love's mysteries became a personal and professional quest for us. Our desire is to understand and to explain love's mysteries as best as mere mortals can.

Our goal is not to overdissect the mysteries of oneness between a man and a woman. To overexamine the properties of love, in order to strive for perfection, would almost lend irreverence to its magic. Rather, our goal is to allow the qualities of soul mating to be studied and examined, in an effort to make long-term love more comprehensible. It is our hope that this comprehension will make love more attainable for those who so bravely seek it.

In the last two decades Tom and I have read books, taken courses, and attended countless seminars on the topic of marriage. Although all of them have been helpful, as a married couple working in the field of marriage counseling, we were left wanting or, more accurately, longing. One was too practical, the other too trite, perhaps another too mystical and some downright impossible!

1

I remember one particular theorist who presented his work at a seminar using himself and his starry-eyed wife to demonstrate his magical communication techniques. There they were—the Barbie and Ken of the marriage counseling scene. She was from an upper-middle-class religious family, and he was descended from great Christian orators and philosophers. How inadequate we felt beside these two partners, with their great foundations, discussing their ideas of marital bliss. Boy, did we ever feel like fish out of water. Our familial histories of divorce alone were enough to disqualify us from ever achieving this goal of "matrimonial nirvana."

Where, we asked ourselves, were the fearful, the neurotic, the tired, the poor, the huddled masses yearning to be wed? Where were those honest souls, desiring to love and to be loved, baggage and all? Where could real hurting souls go to find intimacy? These are the people we want in a communication seminar—the yellers, the screamers, the criers, the blamers. These are the real men and women of the marital trenches. These wounded souls with broken dreams from poor role models and sagging foundations from childhood wounds are the real heroes of the marital battlefield—not Barbie and Ken. These people are the ones who are really aware that they are in the midst of a war, thrilling and terrible at the same time. These precious, brave sojourners are the ones we want to see in a marriage workshop—the ones who need to find the strength and resources to love their partner when it just gets too hard.

Yes, Barbie and Ken's ideas are noteworthy, but many of us wounded birds feel that we are crippled, even as we start this journey. We do not know how to deal with intimacy and one-ness—and most of the time, it just scares us.

Through our years of education, experience, and study, we have set out to determine what makes marriages work and what causes them to fail. In doing so, we have developed several techniques and exercises that are designed to fortify marriages. We began using these techniques in our own relationship, as well as in our private Christian counseling practice. Teaching them at various seminars we call Soul Healers Workshops became an offshoot of this effort. As the demand grew, we expanded our format to include church groups, small-group fellowships, Bible studies, and Sunday school classes. People wanted more. They requested an instructional guide or training manual to follow as they were learning how to do the exercises successfully. This manuscript was born out of our desire to meet their needs.

It was originally penned with hurting couples in mind, designed specifically for those who could not communicate—distant and even separated couples. We felt a particular affinity with the wounded hearts, the handicapped masses, and the fearful plenty. Eventually we began to see that healthy couples found the information helpful in enhancing their already intact marriages. Singles used it to develop their relationship skills. This material has been developed for anyone who has been married, is married, or wants to be married.

Salted throughout this book are case studies of actual couples who have learned to use these techniques successfully. Their names and details have been altered to protect their anonymity. We are grateful for the faith they have displayed in our work as they trusted us with their sacred souls. These precious couples truly honored us by their participation and success. To further obscure their identities and to bring some levity to otherwise serious content, we have used names of television couples who were popular in the fifties and sixties. You may enjoy a break now and then and find this both interesting and entertaining as you make the connection.

While the book is written mostly from my (Bev's) perspective, you will often see the words *we*, *us*, and *our*. This is because Tom and I are one. Many of the ideas and theories are ours, developed together consciously and oftentimes unconsciously as a result of our own marital and professional journeys. We have spent many hours staffing cases and discussing aspects of marriage, not only to help the couples we work with but also to help our own marriage. The material you are about to read is a compilation of both of our ideas, thoughts, and musings. I am only the willing spokesperson for this duo.

This book has been written for those brave souls who desire active duty in the war of love and marriage and who still have enough determination, faith, and hope to make it fruitful. For those courageous souls who set sail on this treacherous yet unavoidable voyage, we bid you God's understanding and his infinite wisdom as you read the "map" that lies ahead.

Let us journey together now, with our shaky foundations and wounded hearts to discover a long-term, heart-satisfying, soul-healing love. We are proud and thrilled to have you traveling with us.

Chapter 1

The Purpose of Love

Nowadays if a couple makes it past twenty-five years of marriage, they are looked on as heroes or relational icons. Society sees them as really lucky, extremely laid-back, or just plain deaf, dumb, and blind. Happy, fulfilling, long-term relationships are becoming increasingly rare. Divorce in our society is at an all-time high. Marriage counseling practices are booming with couples who just can't seem to grasp love's magic. What is this thing called love? How do some couples seem to get it right while others stumble from relationship to relationship? Is love just a mystical experience that finds some lucky souls and leaves others barren and longing? Many songs are written about love, and movies make romantic love their primary objective. Even after destroying the villain and eradicating his entire cyberspace mainframe, our hero still has time to find the love of his life. Being the perennial romantic, I would like to believe that true love would find me worthy of its bounty, and that I would find that mystical love that would heal all of my life's ills and quiet all of my internal pain. In the past eighteen years as a marital and family therapist, I have studied love from many aspects and have found that true love is far less mystical than our culture or the media portray. I have come to a solemn but very real conclusion: True love is hard work.

Long-term, committed love is the hardest work our souls will ever undertake. Like many other great gifts, love has its sacrifices and its responsibilities. Contrary to what movies, romance novels, and almost-forgotten fairy tales have depicted for years, love is not easy. Loving the soul of another human being and receiving his or her love in return is an awesome challenge. It takes insight, fortitude, wisdom, and skill. Love doesn't come magically or all at once. It takes time and patience. "Happily ever after" requires arduous effort.

If love is so hard, why do we want it so badly? The answer is simple: because we do. The greatest need for the human soul is to love and to be loved. We all want to feel love's warmth wrap around us. Many of us secretly hunger for it, while others search more overtly. Nevertheless, the goal is still the same: to find true love, to find a love that heals the soul, to find a love that lasts. Although love has its mystical qualities and is very difficult to understand, we believe that it is attainable for all those who bravely knock on its door.

A Familiar Tale

We remember two young, naive college kids some twenty years ago who embarked on this course of long-term love, not knowing where the winds of fortune would take them. Their story may strike a cord of familiarity in many of you. It begins with a young girl growing up in a small, backward southern town. She spent a good bit of her childhood watching her parents' bitter, violent fights. When she went to bed at night, she would put her hands over her ears and secretly pray that no one would be seriously maimed, disfigured, or dead when she awoke. Most of the time she was lucky, but there were a few close calls. Her mother, an adult child of an alcoholic, would scream accusations of indiscretions at her father, who would retaliate.

When the dust settled in the morning, the girl would tiptoe through the mangled house, which looked much like the aftermath of a hurricane, and secretly vow that she would never have a marriage like this. She didn't know how she was going to avoid it, but she was not going to live like those two. This would never happen to her!

Things worsened in her home. Her father finally left her mother, breaking the young girl's heart. Her mom grew hard and bitter. Her dad married a much younger woman and moved away, making visitations less frequent. Her mom went to work full-time, leaving four latchkey waifs to sail parentless on the sea of the 1960s. The girl's brother found peace, love, Flower Power, and, unfortunately, drugs. She found religion. With religion as her bastion of hope, she set out to make things different. She knew this was her answer. God would never let her have a marriage like her parents. His word speaks of harmony, commitment, fidelity, and unconditional love. With the help of her faith, she would not repeat her parents' mistakes. She would be different. She would find her true love. Her dreams would come true.

On the other side of the United States, in contemporary California, a young boy was having struggles of his own. Raised in a church-going family with a church elder for a father and a Sunday school teacher for a mother, he was devastated to discover that his family was breaking up due to his father's chronic adultery. This was the man he had idolized as a child. This man had disappointed and betrayed him. His family was falling apart and there was nothing he could do about it. His parents managed to stay together (for the children's sake) until the boy graduated from college and then they divorced. Disillusioned and hopeless, the young man set out for redemption through a life of Christian service, vowing that he would live his life differently. With God's help, he would not repeat his parents' pattern. Unlike them, he would find his life's love. He would find his soul mate.

And so it was that the young hillbilly girl from Tennessee found the contemporary boy from California. His parents divorced after twenty-six years and hers after only eleven, leaving both with the same scars and fears that many grown kids of divorced parents possess. They were united with the hope and dream that they were going to handle marriage differently from their parents. They were also afraid. It was with this hope, and with this fear, that their relationship began.

This story is very familiar to Tom and me. The names have been changed to protect the innocent and the guilty. This is our story. Now, some twenty years later, we are still in awe of love's mysteries. We have found love to be both mystical and literal, both abstract and concrete, both verb and noun. We are, above all, grateful that it found us worthy of its magnificent rewards. These rewards did not come without a great price, and that is why we wanted to write this book. We chose to write about soul-healing love not because we are such a great example of matrimony but rather because we are not. Almost despite our family histories of divorce, abuse, and dysfunction, our idiosyncratic personality quirks, and our weird phobic predispositions, we have managed to survive marriage (sometimes just barely) for some twenty years.

Our journey has brought us through moves, career changes, poverty, riches, two beautiful children, several adored pets, and even a frightening brush with death. Currently in midlife, we have compassion for those who wonder why everything wrinkles, sags, bulges, and generally refuses to function at this stage of life's game. We have felt the famous loss of energy and life passion that goes with midlife crisis. As marriage and family therapists, we see this not only in each other but also in our clients.

Now, don't get the wrong idea here. Just because we are both therapists does not mean we have any better edge against the demons of our hurtful pasts. In fact, it can be quite embarrassing to slide into unhealthy, dysfunctional communication patterns when we spend all day instructing others not to do so. Here again, almost despite ourselves, we have learned from our own experiences and would like to pass some of this wisdom on to the next generation of lovers. Maybe because of some of these lessons, we can ease the fear and pain that often accompany intimacy and instill the hope in this generation that true love is an attainable reality. We want couples to learn that true love is less magic and more hard work than the media would like us to believe, that falling in love is different from staying in love, and that loving someone means wanting to heal the pain of their soul, as they in turn heal yours. True soul-healing love is possible, even for those who have repeatedly lost at love or who have grown up in homes of dysfunction and divorce.

Love's Disillusionment

Ken was one of those adult kids of divorce and dysfunction. He came into our office after his third marriage fell apart. Ken had knocked on love's door many times. He came to therapy to get help in dealing with the pain of his breakup and to learn about his relationship patterns so he could "find one that would work." Ken had many doubts and fears about love and marriage, but he was willing to learn.

I remember one day he shared a joke that he had heard from Rodney Dangerfield. Ken could really relate to this feeling. The comedian said he wasn't going to get married again, he was just going to find a woman who hated him and buy her a big house. Ken wasn't the only client we have treated in therapy who shared this disillusioned opinion of marriage. More and more people have found themselves in Ken's shoes. At first he said the standard lines, "Maybe I just haven't found the right one," and "I guess I am just unlucky at love." After a while, however, Ken began to see that true love was a skill that had to be learned. Eventually his hard work took the place of bad luck, and ability took the place of chance. With time and effort, he became a successful lifetime partner.

Some people are victims of divorce. They see that their marriages are in trouble, and they do everything in their power to try to repair them, but their partners are not willing to try. Fred and Wilma were such a couple. They had been married for thirty-three years. Fred was a leader in the community and taught a young couples Sunday school class for some twenty years. Many couples looked up to him as an example because of his excellent tutelage on matrimony. Then Fred left his wife and two grown children and moved in with Betty, his twenty-seven-year-old divorced secretary. Wilma begged Fred to come to marriage counseling, but he refused and their marriage ended.

Ward and June had been married for fourteen years and had three beautiful children. Then one day June announced that she thought marriage was suffocating, and that she was not in love with Ward anymore. She wanted out. They came to a few sessions of marriage counseling, but June dropped out very early. Ward continued to come and bring their children to us for counseling. I'll never forget the pain on their eight-year-old son's face when he said he wanted to die because life as he knew it would never be the same. A month earlier, June had left Ward and the kids and joined an archeological dig in a graduate school in New Mexico. We still see the children on occasion, and they report that their mom has had several serial relationships with younger men, but she is not happy and still does not have the love she wants. As marital therapists, we wonder if this was an unnecessary divorce.

Accounts like these send shock waves throughout people's families, friends, churches, and communities. The ripple effect impacts the community for many seasons to come. Tom and I see these kinds of disheartened lovers every day. They come in all shapes and sizes, and so do their emotional wounds and hurts. But they all share one common characteristic—they desperately want this soul-healing love and just can't seem to find it.

As therapists we may never completely understand love's disillusionment, but we do hope to shed some light on the Lord's purpose of true love. In trying to understand God's design, we as finite creatures may be able to help others find the love they so desperately want and need. This understanding may strengthen husbands and wives and enable them to become committed partners.

Where Love Starts

> For this cause a man shall leave his father and mother, and shall cleave to his wife; and they shall become one flesh. And the man and his wife were both naked and were not ashamed (Gen 2:24–25).

To understand the design of long-term love, we only have to begin at the beginning. Genesis gives us a clear idea of what marriage is about. First, men and women are to leave. This leaving is not merely a moving out from under the roof or authority of previous families in order to establish a new unit. It is also a turning away from our family's influence and what they have consciously and unconsciously imprinted upon our psyches. In Scripture we see that marriage is designed so couples turn away from the functions and dysfunctions of the past to establish a new healing love in marriage. As we move from the joys and scars of the past to this new love, we will cleave to each other. The Hebrew word picture here is talking about soldering, much like a welder would solder two metals together. When the craftsman has completed his final product, the observer cannot discern where one metal alloy leaves off and the other begins.

To complement this illustration, let's look at the term *synergy*. This is a term used more in the context of chemical reaction than relationships. Synergy is defined as the interaction of elements that when combined produce a total effect that is greater than the sum of its parts. The true love that God has designed for his children puts the hearts and souls of two individuals together and merges them with a synergistic energy that produces a union that is greater than the sum of its two parts. It is this cleaving that merges human souls into oneness.

This soul-merging oneness is not to be confused with how women in the 1950s found their identity in their husbands. Because these women did not have a sense of who they were on their own, they became appendages of their husbands. In this type of oneness, wives' opinions were stated by their husbands, and their roles were dictated by culture and society. Since our culture looked more favorably on men at the time, women did not have the freedom to choose ways in which they wished to serve in their marriages. This created a severe identity crisis for many women. Mutual submission, as discussed in the Ephesians 5 passage, was rarely achieved at this point in the development of marriage. These women with low self-esteem needed identities, which their husbands provided. Although the two were considered one (ask her what she thought, and he'd answer), this is not the glorious oneness we speak of in this text.

This same soul-healing oneness is also not to be confused with the *codependency* touted in the 1980s, in which women and men met their need for improved self-esteem by overinvolving themselves in the needs of others. Codependents live other people's lives by controlling, enabling, or caretaking. A common example of codependency is the enabling wife of the alcoholic, who lives to make her husband sober, while her very helping leads him to drink more. There's a saying that when the codependent dies, everyone else's life passes before his or her eyes. Although a codependent wife thinks that her caretaking love will heal her mate, her low self-esteem and misunderstanding of true oneness create more distance than soul healing.

True Soul-Healing Love

Caring for the soul of another—true soul-healing love—does not require merging identities or codependency. It means learning to accept and love ourselves as God does, then taking that awesome God-given love and acceptance and willingly bestowing it upon our partner. Think for a moment about the love of God. Meditate on the greatness of this gift. God loves us with all of our warts and flaws.

Many Christians we see in counseling believe in their head that God loves them, but they do not feel this love in their heart. These perplexed souls do not see how God could accept them with all of their defects. As a result, they don't love and accept themselves. These individuals judge themselves harshly and without mercy. Often they judge their partners with the same harshness as well.

People with soul wounds have a harder time believing that they are lovable. Tom and I are two such people. Soul wounds are those hurts and pains inflicted upon the psyche that leave emotional scars. Rejection, abandonment, criticism, abuse, and neglect are types of soul wounds. This subject will be covered more thoroughly in Chapter 3. These hurts cause us to feel inadequate and unworthy of love. God's unconditional love heals our wounds. His love restores us to wholeness. We then can become merciful and loving to ourselves and subsequently to our spouses.

In summary, soul-healing love has five basic parts:

1. God loves us unconditionally, and this love heals our soul wounds and restores us to wholeness.

2. This love helps us see ourselves through God's eyes and learn to love ourselves as God does, imperfections and all.

3. Because we feel loved and lovable, we can allow God's grace and love to spill over onto our spouse. We can see our spouse through God's eyes and love him or her as God does.

4. Soul-healing love brings about trust, vulnerability, and sharing that bonds us as a couple and merges us into a deep oneness.

5. This oneness replicates the oneness we feel with God; therefore, our love for our spouse and his or her love for us also restores us both to wholeness. Just as the love of

God is soul healing, so the love between a husband and a wife is soul healing as well.

This love is given to our mate out of our appreciation and gratitude to God because of his love. It is in response to God's love that we love our partner. Soul-healing love comes out of our fullness, and our healthy self-esteem, not out of our lack.

God's Love for Us — Our Example

This soulful love of ourselves, as God loves us, gives us the energy to merge with the soul of another without the fear that we will be controlled, suffocated, or abused. As we become familiar with our own wounds, personality quirks, flesh patterns, and human frailties, we also become familiar with those of our spouse. We learn to understand and even appreciate all of the aspects of both souls, the good and the evil, the light and the shadow. Rather than entering into a lifetime commitment with the thought of what we can gain in the forefront of our minds, we enter with the notion that we are going to love our mate as God loves us. We also begin to allow God's unconditional love, or agape, to penetrate us and fill us. This enables us to see ourselves through his eyes, as his creation. The outgrowth is that we are now energized to love ourselves and our partners unconditionally.

Because God loves us, we can love another. Healing our past hurts, accepting those things we cannot change, and forgiving our perpetrators becomes a conscious and an unconscious goal. As our soul's journey continues, it is fueled by a desire to share this love with others. This energy finds another soul, merges with it, and begins the process of knowing and being known by another. We learn to accept each other, baggage and all. The pain of our past injures our mate just as it once emotionally injured us. Healing our mate's wounds also heals our own. We desire to love our mate, and we help our mate love himself or herself. We want to share God's unconditional love with our partner because we have so richly experienced it as one of God's special children. John 4:11 says, "Beloved, if God so loved us, we ought also to love one another." As both husbands and wives bask in God's love, they will strongly desire to share it with each other. It is from God's wonderful love for us that soul-healing love is born.

Love is reciprocal. When you give soul-healing love to your spouse, the energy of this union has a reciprocal effect. Because you are loved unconditionally, you will spontaneously desire to go beyond the usual self-serving rituals of love to a more transcendent agape for your mate. This sets up an endless cycle of giving and receiving. Selfishness is replaced with a spontaneous reciprocity of caring. You cannot outgive your mate and vice versa.

Love is learning. As you begin the journey as a soul-healing partner, you will learn a great deal about your past emotional hurt and pain (or your soul wounds), and you will learn about what has wounded your partner. You will realize that much of this pain accounts for both of your coping styles and relationship struggles today. In fact, much of the pain you inflict upon each other in your marriage is a direct or indirect result of the pain you have experienced earlier in life. Once you realize the woundedness in both yourself and your spouse, you can then move beyond the typical power struggles that couples have and learn to love each other as friends and lovers, imperfections and all. This is not merely a toleration of each other's warts and scars, but an empathy and understanding of your mate's soul that inspires a deep care. This love allows you to wait patiently and prayerfully for your spouse's spiritual, soulful transformation. You do not ignore the wounds your mate inflicts upon you in denial, but you no longer retaliate in a very unhealthy or "unhealing" manner.

In loving your mate with a soul-healing love, you will strongly desire to hear about the wounds of his or her past. In return, your partner will patiently listen as you share painful stories of your childhood. Both of you will develop empathy that will allow you to experience your partner's pain as if it were your own.

Love is *koinonia*. The Greek word *koinonia* was used a great deal in the Jesus movement in the 1960s and 1970s to describe Christian sharing. Many churches picked it up as a catch phrase for Bible studies and fellowship groups. The true meaning of the word actually applies here, however. The word *koinonia* is defined as "mutual empathy." What it means is that when your husband or wife shares his or her pain with you, you feel it as well. You respond as if the same pain is also happening to you. This koinonia merges both of your souls into one. When your partner's soul aches, your soul will bleed, and vice versa. His or her wounds become your own, and healing him or her will eventually heal you as well.

Love your mate as you love yourself. Ephesians 6:28 commands husbands to "love their wives as they love their own body. He who loves his wife loves himself." The Living Bible says that husbands should love their wives as a part of themselves, "For since a man and his wife are now one, a man is really doing himself a favor and loving himself when he loves his wife." If we as couples would really heed this wisdom, it would truly transform marriages today.

God's Plan for Us

What a marvelous plan God intended. Two souls united with synergistic passion. The energy this creates brings healing. Because of this mutual sharing, you are really doing yourself a favor by loving your partner and vice versa. By giving to your partner, you also receive. By listening to your partner's soul, yours is heard. When you tell your partner what you need and he or she gives it to you, the giving of this gift will not only heal you, but his or her soul will be healed as a result. This mutual reciprocity is God's glorious design for marriage. In leaving and cleaving and becoming one, couples are exemplifying the Great Omnipotent Soul Healer, Jesus Christ. "This is love: not that we loved God, but that he loved us, and sent his son as an atoning sacrifice for our sins" (1 Jn 4:10).

God in his infinite wisdom designed a love between a husband and a wife that replicates his own sacrificial love for his children. By seeking to become a soul healer to yourself and to your partner, lover, and friend, you can become Christ-like. As you model Christ's loving essence to your mate's wounded soul, you are giving that person the greatest present he or she could ever receive. Only the creator of the universe could design a marvelous reciprocity of sharing such as this.

The notion of such loving and caring between partners almost boggles the mind. As a child growing up in a dysfunctional family, I never dreamed this kind of love was possible. Many of my clients share this skepticism about love, maybe because they also were raised in similar homes. Here is a story of two fellow skeptics.

Jim and Karen's Story

Jim and Karen were one such skeptical couple. Jim swaggered into the counseling office and introduced himself with a hearty handshake. Karen, also alive and bubbly, followed holding little eight-year-old Jimmy's hand. After the rest of the introductions were made, Karen began telling me why they had come. Jimmy was just about to be suspended from school because of his disruptive behavior. He was not applying himself in class, and he was getting into fights on the playground. Since Jimmy went to a small private school, these kinds of behavior problems were not tolerated. The principal gave Jimmy and his family one last chance before expelling him and sent them to our counseling office.

It is typical in the first session to get a complete family history from both parents, so I began my investigation. "Are your parents still living, Jim? Is there any history of alcoholism in either your parents or grandparents?"

"What?" Jim exclaimed. "I thought we were here to talk about my son. Why are you asking me all these questions about my parents? What do my parents have to do with Jimmy failing school?" he asked skeptically.

I began to explain to Jim, "They have everything to do with who you are as a person and who you have become as a parent, and therefore, they have had a great direct and indirect effect on your son."

Jim gave Karen the cynical eye-roll I have seen so often from parents in therapy. Karen looked at him as if to say, "Please, give this a try," so Jim continued.

It did not take me long to put the pieces of this family's history together. Jim and Karen were both raised in military families. Karen's father was an alcoholic who began drinking heavily when he retired. Karen was only eleven years old when this happened.

Jim admitted that his father drank heavily, but he couldn't say whether or not he was an alcoholic. Both of their mothers were described as compliant, passive women, who were dominated by their husbands. This often happens in military homes. As you can see, Jim and Karen selected mates with complementary or similar childhood wounds.

I asked each person how they were disciplined when they were children. Once again I got the skeptical look from Jim. By this time, Karen had a look of her own. She cut her eyes over to Jim with as much force as she could muster. Her look told Jim to leave his skepticism at the door. I was winning Karen over.

Karen began first, telling me that her father was critical and demanding. As she continued, her voice grew softer, and her thoughts more pensive, as if she were seeing in her mind's eye what she had experienced as a child. This phenomenon often happens in therapy. The person looks back into their past and envisions childhood happenings. These happenings are complete with the emotions that were felt at that time. It is not uncommon to see a grown person weeping like a child when he or she remembers the abuse of their childhood. This occurrence has been given many names from flashbacks to retroflection. In our practice, we call them *regressive reflections*. Regressive reflections are extremely important in showing clients how they deal with current family relationships. Writer Carlos Santayana once said, "Those who forget the past are condemned to repeat it." This can also be true for those who painfully remember it.

As Karen began to regressively reflect the experiences in her childhood, she wept quietly. Jim became very uncomfortable and began squirming in his seat. With her voice shaking, Karen painted a painful picture of her father's unhealthy dealings with his children. As the middle child of three girls, Karen seemed to get more of her dad's wrath than her sisters.

"So you see, Bev," she said, "this is why we came. I don't want Jim and me to repeat my parents' mistakes." Karen sucked back her tears with a little embarrassment and looked appealingly at Jim.

Jim's discomfort was evident as we turned our attention to him.

"Now I know my dad drank," said Jim, " but I don't believe he was as bad as Karen's dad. He did have high expectations of us and he was a perfectionist, but he just wanted the best for his children. Dad grew up poor and he wanted us to have what he couldn't. As the older of two boys, I guess he expected more from me than my brother, and he was strict. But I can't remember him really, what you would call, abusing me—"

"Don't you remember," Karen interrupted, "when he hit you right before he sent you to military school?" Karen looked at me and said, "Jim told me about this when we were dating. There were other instances too, when I think Jim's dad was too harsh in disciplining him." Her misty-eyed look encouraged me to keep going. She seemed to be saying nonverbally that I was on to something.

I did keep going, but I could tell Jim was fearful of something. It was as if he had something to hide. He seemed shut down, determined not to show any emotion, as if he was just going to report the facts, not feelings.

I then asked the two of them how they disciplined Jimmy. Jim looked really uncomfortable then. Karen began to weep softly. As she spoke, it became apparent that she was unhappy about how Jim had been treating Jimmy.

She felt that Jim was abusive to little Jimmy in an effort to get him to obey. She also said that she feared Jim had adopted some of his own father's extremely critical per-fectionism in raising his children. Karen went on to say that *she* even felt unloved by Jim at times because he was hurting one of her most precious possessions, her son.

"If he loved us, he would not treat us this way! I even secretly doubt if I can stay in this marriage when Jim treats Jimmy like this," she said.

Jim looked shocked, but guilty. He realized that he was not only hurting his son with his impatient abusive tendencies, he was also hurting his wife. He was con-cerned that his family was so hurt by him, and that Karen felt that he was becoming like his father. The idea of him ever becoming like that sent cold chills down his spine. It was hard for Jim to see that he was doing some of the very things that he despised in his father. He had a great deal of guilt about this. This guilt worked to his and his family's advantage, however, because he made another appointment right away, and began to put his faith in Christian therapy to help heal them.

As the weeks went by, Jim and Karen revealed to each other many scenes of childhood abuse. They learned how to comfort each other and lend support to each other's souls as they shared their pain. This bonded them in a way that they had not previously known. It wasn't easy, but they allowed God's love and forgiveness to heal the wounds that they had intentionally and unintentionally inflicted upon each other. Through time, they became soul-healing lovers.

As for Jimmy, we were all amazed. As his mom and dad grew closer, he became much more peaceful and his behavior was more stable. We spent some time in therapy teaching Jim and Karen more refined parenting tools and teaching Jimmy the logical consequences of his actions. Jimmy was also tested for learning disabilities, and we discovered that he had attention deficit disorder, which we began to treat through tutoring and medication. Upon further investigation, we discovered that Jim also had ADD. He learned that he had always compensated for this by overachievement and perfectionism. This awareness helped Jim understand and better relate to his son.

It has been many years since this family committed themselves to becoming soul healers. We still bump into them periodically. Jim and Karen's relationship continues to flourish and is a blessing to our own souls. Jimmy is now doing quite well in school. He is six feet two inches tall and weighs 220 pounds, and plays offensive and defensive tackle for his school's football team. In the stands sit his two greatest fans—his mother and father.

For this kind of soul transformation to take place, Jim and Karen had to begin to develop a clear understanding of the soul. We have found that this understanding is necessary for all clients who wish to become soul healers. It is vitally important then to discern the purpose of the soul. We give our clients what we call a "working definition of the soul." The next chapter is devoted to an understanding of that definition.

Chapter 2

The Purpose of the Soul

The proper place to start, in training soul healers, is to learn as much about the soul as possible. Tom and I have found that this is an awesome task, and one that can only be completed with much reverence and respect.

Many philosophers, theologians, and psychologists have discussed the soul. Although Tom and I do not claim to have their abundant knowledge, we do feel the need to develop a working definition of the soul, so that you can fully grasp the depth of what we are trying to convey. The task set before us is to stretch ourselves philosophically, with much humility, to define *soul*.

The soul is the principle of life. It is that core energy or life energy that is both the invisible and the sentient element of human beings. It is the spiritual part of humans, or the moral aspect, believed to survive in the life hereafter, which means it is subject to happiness or misery in the life to come. The soul is the true, real emotional nature of a human being. It is the substance or essence of who he or she is.[1]

Grolier's Encyclopedia defines the soul as the spiritual part of human beings that animates their physical existence and survives death. *Grolier's* goes on to say that *soul* is a term rarely used with precise definition in philosophy, religion, or common life.[2] As we began to research a clear definition of soul, we were inclined to agree.

In Scripture, the Greek word for soul is *psuche*. This is close to our English version of *psyche*, meaning "breath," or "breath of life." Since God made the soul as the central aspect of man that is most like him, the soul is probably the most God-like part of the human psyche. The soul's God-like nature enables it to be capable of great depth and caring. It is this aspect of the soul that can merge with a partner and create the oneness discussed in Ephesians: "For this reason a man shall leave his father and mother, and be united to his wife, and the two will be one flesh" (5:31). Being aware of the capabilities of the soul, as well as its frailties, can help couples achieve the oneness God has designed for them.

Vine's Expository Dictionary of New Testament Words differentiates *soul* from *spirit* by clarifying that spirit is man's higher nature, while soul is man's lower element. Thus things that are said to be sensed or felt in one's spirit may not necessarily be felt in the soul as well. *Vine's* sees the soul as the day-in and day-out essence of life, the inhaling and exhaling of one's being.

One aspect of defining and caring for the soul is what John and Paula Sanford call "the healing of memories." This term was made popular in Christian counseling circles during the last two decades. The Sanfords' work discusses the transformation of the inner person, which is a soul-cleansing, soul-healing process that helps mend the soul from past abuses in order to allow it to soar freely and to grow spiritually (191ff).

The Sanfords make the point that healing negative memories from the past can prepare the soul to worship God and to better love humankind. We see people everyday in our counseling center who have little or no awareness of the hurt and pain that is in their souls. These people have a great deal of trouble in their relationships, and they do not seem to understand why. Some are not Christians, so it is more understandable that they would be oblivious to aspects of the soul. But Christians can have a wealth of knowledge about their souls because the Creator of the Universe inhabits them and wants to use them for his will and purpose. If this awareness is missing, they may need inner healing.

In his modern-day classic, *The Care of the Soul*, Thomas Moore says, "Tradition teaches that soul lies midway between understanding and unconsciousness, and that instrument is neither the mind nor the body, but imagination....Fulfilling work, rewarding relationships, personal power, and relief from symptoms are all gifts of the soul" (17). Moore implies such reverence and respect for the soul that he discusses it as if it has its own intelligence or sense of power, often referring to it simply as *soul*. He quotes psychology as a secular science, but says that care of the soul is a sacred art (xiii–xiv).

The purpose of this book is not to come up with the perfect definition of the soul. We will leave that to theologians and modern-day mystics. We are merely trying to find a clear, working definition of soul to help you begin the incredible voyage of discovering yourself and your partner. We may never fully understand the complexities or the mysteries of the soul in this lifetime. For some thirty years, we have both studied and we are still perplexed by its intricacies and awed by its power. For the purpose of this book, however, we will refer to the soul as "a man and woman's essence, the true and basic nature, the life breath or life energy."

Thus, the soul is what renders life and vitality to humans. The soul is our vivacity, our verve, our energy. It is the resulting life constituted in the individual, and the body is the material organism that is animated by it. For the purpose of this book, the term *soul* will refer to the "real, true self, which will include emotions, will, appetites, and memories."

The Soul Is Vulnerable

Because the soul contains emotions, appetites, and memories, it is vulnerable to pain and hurt. Emotional hurts from the past can have a great impact on the soul. These hurts or soul wounds can offer a wealth of knowledge about how a person relates to all aspects of life, and how he or she interacts in love relationships.

To develop soul-healing love for each other, couples will have to explore their souls. This is a very difficult task because many people do not wish to face the ugly, dark parts of themselves. Seeing one's soul for what it really is, the good and the bad, is extremely hard. Perhaps it is even harder for Christians, who are taught every Sunday to be good and righteous and, therefore, feel guilty when they see their sinful nature. This grace-less guilt causes many people not to face their sin and deal with it. They hide from the truth about themselves. They do not admit that their sin natures even exist. When they do stumble and sin, they quickly acknowledge their sin and then repress it. Thus, they never have a chance to confess sin and learn about the unhealthy aspects of their souls in order to heal them.

Thomas Moore said, "Moralism is one of the most effective shields against the soul, protecting us from its intricacy" (*Care* 59). If a person is too moralistic or judgmental about his or her own soul, he or she will be equally judgmental, if not more so, about his or her spouse's soul. Getting to know one's own soul and loving it as God does will help a person give and receive love in relationships.

The Soul and Fear

What happens when one wounded soul sails aimlessly upon the sea of relationships and comes in contact with another repressed, wounded soul? The books, songs, and movies speak to us of romantic bliss that lasts happily ever after—two lost souls joyfully found, never to suffer again! This is not what statistics show us. The average length of a relationship is only four years, so happily-ever-after keeps getting shorter all of the time (Toufexis 50).

We are seeing more marriages break up these days, and we are also seeing more commitment phobia in singles. These young urbanites are dating less and waiting longer to marry. Perhaps these singles are being more selective in the matrimonial process, but the high divorce rate coupled with the lower pleasure index of married couples indicate that fear may be the real culprit here. These young would-be partners see marriage as a jail sentence, rather than as a life-enhancing commitment. They are afraid marriage will diminish their quality of life, and rather than take that chance, they remain single. There are those, however, who choose to marry and, in ignorance, become frightened with their choice.

Commitment Equals Chaos

Commitment has a way of causing paranoia in many souls. In his book, *Getting the Love You Want*, Harville Hendrix says that committed love brings out the archaic fear of death in people. Lovers move to a very infantile place in their unconscious as they try to learn to trust each other. Hendrix states that couples usually have a major conflict within seventy-two hours of making a commitment (65ff). Many times, this is because their ability to trust has been fractured. People who grew up in homes where their caregivers were not reliable can have problems with trust. Perhaps their parent or parents were alcoholics or worked all the time. Maybe their father or mother was away for a long period. These situations can wreak havoc on a person's ability to build trust in relationships.

Since the basis of a romantic relationship requires the soul to trust, these people are consciously or unconsciously fearful of making this kind of commitment. Falling in love reminds them of their primary love relationship (that of their parents), and this scares them to death. They have difficulty giving their partners all the privileges of their love, because with those privileges comes the power to be hurt as well. These wounded souls are all too aware that if they fall in love, their partner then has a great deal of power over them, and this is scary. One could say that these people have "broken trusters."

Basic Trust

Those of you who took Psychology 101 will remember Harry Harlow's study of monkeys. Harlow had two groups of baby monkeys. Both groups were given surrogate mothers. One surrogate mother monkey was made of cloth. Although she could give her babies warmth, she could not feed them. The other mother monkey was made of wire; however, she was rigged to be able to nurse the baby monkeys. Even though the baby monkeys could not get food from the warm cloth mother, they still preferred her over the cold wire surrogate. As the study showed, many of the monkeys failed to thrive under the care of the wire monkey.

I will never forget the picture in my psychology book of two baby monkeys clinging to each other tightly, filled with fear and insecurity. Harlow dubbed these monkeys "together-together monkeys." The outcome of his study showed that monkeys (as well as humans) need warmth and security, not just food, in order to learn what he called "basic trust." Without basic trust, insecurity grows, and all future relationships suffer (43ff).

Many of us go into relationships like those clinging baby monkeys who have shattered "trusters." Oftentimes I have said that I was raised by a "wire mother" who, because of her own soul wounds, was not capable of loving me. A lot of the people we see in counseling share similar feelings about their parents. With this kind of upbringing, we enter into committed relationships at a disadvantage. With all of our hearts, we want to love and be loved, yet this causes us so much angst that we have a hard time embracing it. Getting the love we so desperately want scares us to death. It arouses all of our suspicions and anxieties. It is both desired and feared. Our anxiety levels are high because unconditional love is so unfamiliar to us.

Wish Fulfillment Theory

Sigmund Freud developed what he called the "wish fulfillment theory," in which he postulated that with the fulfillment of every wish comes the fear that it will not be granted again. Thus, getting what you wish for causes anxiety (142). This is especially true when it comes to romantic love because it is man's and woman's deepest and most basic soul need. The fear of that love being taken away after it has been given is equal to the fear of death. People literally fear the destruction of their own soul at the hands of their partner. Thus, it is easy to see not only how people can fear love but also how they become obsessed with the loved one. Stalking, revenge, suicide threats, and other types of unhealthy behaviors are a result of this type of addictive love. These people have identified their former partner with the survival of their very soul.

With such high expectations placed on love, marriage can become a formula for chaos. Many people yield to their anxiety and exit the marriage, only to find themselves repeating the same unhealthy patterns, or continuing to be at risk for further aimless searching on the sea of relationships. These lovers search for the "right one" instead of looking inward to their own souls for the answer. Oftentimes the "right one" is directly in front of them, but a lack of awareness of the soul blinds them to its realization.

As you can see, discovering the purpose of the soul, and understanding the soul's attributes can help individuals learn how to merge into the mysterious oneness that God has intended for his children. Lack of awareness and understanding can thwart this merger. The following is a story of a Christian couple who came into counseling having very little awareness of what the soul was all about.

Greg and Marsha's Soul Exploration

Marsha was a very pleasant, overweight woman who came to our counseling center because she was not able to control her eating. Food had become a compulsion for her. During her first session, she said that she had waited a long time to decide to seek help because Greg, her husband, did not believe in counseling. Whenever she would share her struggles over food with him, he would accuse her of not praying enough for self-control or suggest she study the Bible. Although this hurt Marsha, she was inclined to agree with him. She would then feel bad and try even harder to control her eating. Greg finally agreed that she could go to therapy and that he would accompany her a few times. However, he made it very clear that he was not coming in for himself. He wanted us to know that it was Marsha's problem, not his.

As I was exploring their family histories, I discovered that both Greg and Marsha were the oldest in their families. Marsha had two younger brothers, and Greg had a younger brother and a younger sister. Both described their parents as strict and controlling. Both rebelled as teens and participated in various counter-cultural activities that caused them a great deal of pain. Neither felt good about their teenage years, and both reported having emotional scars as a result of their rebellious behavior. Here again, we see individuals with similar soul wounds attracted to each other.

Greg and Marsha had met each other fourteen years ago when neither was living a Christian life. After they were married, they continued to live life in the "fast lane," drinking very heavily and using drugs regularly. Marsha quit drinking when she got pregnant, but Greg continued to drink and take drugs.

After the birth of their first child, they decided to try to live a Christian lifestyle. They began to go to church and immediately became involved there. The transformation for Greg was tremendous. He gave up drugs and alcohol. With tears in his eyes, he said that he never wanted to use drugs or drink after that time. Several weeks after his conversion, he also gave up cigarettes and said that he never had the desire to smoke again. Greg gave God the credit for the change that took place in his life. He felt as if his soul was where it needed to be. He was going to church, and living a godly life. What more could he ask for?

Whenever Greg was asked how he gave up such addictive habits, he would, in preacherlike style, say, "I just did it!" Now, although that advice would be good for a Nike advertisement, it was not good for simple church folks who struggled with compulsive behaviors. It was especially damaging to Marsha, who had tried hard to control her eating but had had a very difficult time doing so.

After a while, Marsha began to feel unloved. Greg's judgmental, shaming style was taking its toll on their marriage. When I asked Greg about this, his response was typical of his preacherlike attitude. "Marsha, like most people, just doesn't want to hear the truth about her sin. She wants me to feel sorry and make excuses for her. Well, I can't pity someone who just needs to get a grip on herself and practice some of the fruits of the spirit, like self-control. Marsha wants her 'ears tickled' (to hear what she wants to hear)." This type of response would send Marsha into a tailspin; she would feel hopeless and depressed and eat more.

Marsha told Greg many times that she felt unloved. Greg would call these statements "ridiculous nonsense," and quote Scriptures to her about God's command to him to love his wife and about his determination to obey, no matter what the price. Needless to say, this did not help Marsha feel more loved and cherished by him.

On the other hand, Greg felt that Marsha did not care about him, because he had told her many times that her weight was a problem to him. He felt that she would not lose weight just to spite him. This created a great deal of conflict, especially in their sex life. Marsha struggled with her negative body image and her negative feelings for Greg. The result was she had no sexual desire. Greg, too, had lost sexual desire because he wanted an attractive, shapely spouse who took care of herself. I could quickly see how her issues and his issues worked against each other.

Not only do couples find partners with similar wounds but many of their deepest issues directly impact their mate as well. This occurrence is called *interactivity*. Greg's and Marsha's personal issues were interactive with each other. Further, many of their statements would impact each other's deepest wounds, almost simultaneously. We call these statements *impact statements*. Marsha's weight problem, low self-esteem, and feelings of being unloved interacted with, or impacted, Greg's judgmentalism, compulsive, do-good lifestyle, and feelings of being ignored and disrespected. To heal Marsha's wounds, Greg would have to be willing to interactively heal his own wounds, which caused him to act negatively toward Marsha. Conversely, if Marsha would be willing to heal her compulsive eating wound and learn self-control, this would also heal Greg's feeling of being unloved.

By the time Greg and Marsha came to the counseling center, they were almost convinced that they had married the wrong person because their wounds impacted each other in such a negative way. The truth is that they did indeed pick the right person, *because* their wounds impacted each other in a negative way. Paradoxically speaking, only the partner who has a great amount of interactivity can heal his or her partner's woundedness, and vice versa. We will speak more about interactivity and impact statements in a later chapter.

It was apparent to us that both Greg and Marsha had a very limited idea of soul. They were both ignoring previous soul wounds, which they had repressed or covered up by using drugs and alcohol. This repression caused them to act out in unhealthy ways. They were abusing their own souls and each other's. Both thought that finding salvation was the answer. To quote Marsha, "I thought that once I became a Christian, that was all I needed to do to live a good life." Many new Christians feel that this is the final act for the soul, but it is really just the beginning. God wants to use his awesome power to continue to heal the wounds of our souls and to heal the woundedness of our partners, as they in turn heal us.

Greg and Marsha began to learn about each other. They shared experiences and feelings that they had not shared before. Greg learned that Marsha had been sexually assaulted as a young girl. He sat lovingly and patiently as she shared how painful this was for her, and how it still affected her sexual attitudes and body image. Marsha learned that Greg's father never showed love for him physically or verbally. She listened as he shared how he felt that he had to earn God's love by performing, just as he had had to earn his father's approval. In their sharing, they opened each other's eyes to the pain in their souls. Greg developed empathy and understanding for Marsha, which helped him not to be so judgmental. As Greg became less judgmental and acted in a loving manner toward Marsha, she wanted to reach out and please him. She wanted to be thin, which would please Greg and (she discovered) heal herself. So, by learning about their souls, these two brave sojourners learned to develop a soul-healing love for each other.

Now, years later, Marsha describes Greg as her best friend and her biggest advocate. She still has to maintain discipline about her desire for food, but she feels free from the pain that this compulsive behavior caused her. Greg runs a street ministry, helping homeless people find Christ and get back on their feet. He says regularly that he would not be ministering with the compassion and empathy that he has today, had it not been for all he learned from his soul-healing journey.

Greg and Marsha were excellent mentors of healing to each other. There were things they learned from each other that they could learn from no other person. In therapy they learned that souls are sacred and should be loved and cherished. They gained a new, healthy respect for soul. The interactive nature of the wounds they had inflicted upon each other were transformed into healing balm for their soul pain.

For us to heal our souls and prepare to heal others, we must first examine the environment in which they were formed. Getting in touch with what has happened to us, or finding out what has wounded us, will help heal our souls. Facing our past hurts and wounds also helps us learn to see the wounds of others. Mutual sharing of soul pain can then become a part of our relationships. The next chapter will be dedicated to the arduous, yet rewarding, task of examining the environment of the soul.

Chapter 3

The Soul in Pain

I asked God for strength that I might achieve,
  I was made weak that I might learn to humbly obey.
I asked God for health that I might do greater things,
  I was given infirmity that I might do better things.
I asked God for power that I might have the praise of men,
  I was given weakness that I might feel the need of God.
I asked for all things that I might enjoy life,
  I was given life that I might enjoy all things.
I got nothing that I asked for, but everything that I hoped for,
  Almost despite myself, my unspoken prayers were answered.
I am, among all, most richly blessed!
  —*Author Unknown*

Sandra, a tall, beautiful, blue-eyed blonde, sat in the office crying, with her head in her hands. "I don't know what's the matter with me," she sobbed. "I just keep picking the wrong kind of men. They lie to me and abuse me. I'm just so tired of it all. It seems I always get used by them and then dumped. What's wrong with me? Why can't I find a decent guy?"

Unfortunately, Sandra's dilemma is all too common these days. She came into the counseling center after her second husband had left her for another woman. Both of her husbands had been abusive, and both had trouble keeping jobs. Sandra played the role of caretaker, as well as breadwinner, in both marriages. By the time she came into counseling, she was beginning to see a pattern in her relationships. "This hurts so badly," she would cry. "Please help me just stop the pain. I don't think I can go through this anymore."

It was difficult for Sandra to understand, but for us to help her stop hurting, we first had to encourage her *to hurt*. She had to feel her pain. Like many other wounded people, Sandra was more anxious to stop her soul pain than to understand it. By encouraging her to feel her pain, we showed her how to allow it to be her mentor and teach her about her unhealthy relationship patterns.

Picking these men was not a conscious process on Sandra's part. Her attraction for the wrong kind of men was completely unconscious. Through therapy, she realized that she sought out men who initially portrayed themselves as strong and capable, but seemed in time to show their "true colors"; that is, their weak, dependent side would surface. Eventually, these men would use, abuse, and then abandon her. To assist Sandra, we had to help her understand and deal with her unconscious mind.

The Unconscious Mind

Dr. Larry Crabb, a well-known Christian psychologist, gives us a great illustration of the typical human's awareness of the unconscious mind. Take a blank sheet of notebook paper, and place a small dot in the center of the page. The small dot represents what we know about the unconscious mind, and the great white sea around it represents all that we do not know (56ff). In other words, the vast majority of our experiences, feelings, sensations, and reactions are acted out in relationships, without our conscious awareness. This means that many of our motivations and actions in relationships are not known to us consciously. When we have no clue why we react the way we do in certain situations, the answer may be buried deep in our unconscious mind. As the previous chapter pointed out, our souls, or psyches, are still relatively unexplored.

The notion of exploring the vast unknown regions of the unconscious can be frightening. Any known conscious memories of painful experiences can even deepen our reluctance to start digging through our psyches. Many of us resist looking at previous hurts. We just want to keep them buried.

Sandra shared this sentiment. "Why do I have to relive those painful memories?" she would cry.

I could empathize with her. It is agonizing to look at childhood wounds. I remembered having to face my own painful past, some twenty years earlier.

Fear of Past Pain — A Door of Hope

As a graduate student, I had looked forward to earning my degree in family therapy and then, of course, saving all of humankind. I had decided that I was going to single-handedly heal the brokenhearted and truly set the captives free. (If this sounds a bit messianic, it's because it was.) One day in class, I was asked, much to my surprise, to share some of my own painful childhood memories with the other interns in the graduate program.

"What?" I cried. "Me, relive my childhood? Are you kidding?" I was terrified. "It is done...gone...finished! I've dealt with that stuff a long time ago! I've forgiven my parents for their benign neglect and their blatant abuse! I'm done with all of that!"

I will never forget what my very wise graduate professor said then, "You may be finished with the pain, my dear, but the pain is not finished with you."

She was right, of course. While I had repressed all of the pain of a childhood filled with emotional, psychological, and physical violence, my soul had unconsciously adapted to its wounds by compulsively wanting to heal the pain in everyone else. What I did not realize was that my desire to be a soul healer could only happen as I learned to allow God to heal my own soul.

I decided to give Sandra the same opportunity that I was given those many years earlier: the chance to heal her soul of its painful wounds. This healing journey begins with walking through the door of our unconscious minds and feeling the pain we dread to feel. I knew Sandra would hate doing this, just as I had. Pain's haunting presence had crept into the dark recesses of my soul as if to suffocate me. But I had known that I had to face my dreaded nemesis head-on.

So, I guided Sandra into the dark abyss of her soul's pain. She began to discover something surprising about this journey. She actually saw that pain could be a friend, a positive teaching tool, a wise mentor that illuminated her soul. She learned that pain was not the real culprit. It was the inability to deal with pain that was the problem.

We are given pain as a signal to our psyches, as well as to our bodies, of danger and possible injury. Pain tells us that we need attention. When we cut our finger, it hurts. The pain is a signal that we need to move in a healing direction. When we apply ointment and a bandage, we are on the road to recovery. If our body had not reacted to the pain, we could not have moved toward healing.

The Gift of Pain

Dr. Paul Brand, a physician who worked with lepers for many years, thinks that the greatest problem in treating leprosy is that the afflicted persons have lost their ability to sense and to feel pain. As a result, their tissue can actually deteriorate long before any pain signal is sent to the brain. Lepers can be in serious physical trouble before they are even aware of it. Without feeling the pain, they cannot effectively deal with their disease. For a leper, pain is truly a gift.

As soul healers, we too can learn to see pain as a gift. It can actually be viewed as the soul's signal fire, showing us where we need attention and healing. Pain is not our problem but rather a part of the solution, and therefore, it can become one of our greatest allies.

Society Views Pain Negatively

Feeling our pain can be very foreign in today's modern culture. Our Western civilization has an aversion to dealing with pain and struggle. It is difficult for many people to see the value of grieving or of feeling the losses of the past. We are a generation of instant gratification, fast relief, and microwaved joy. If it hurts, numb it. If it aches, stop it. If it's broken, throw it out. And yet, it is amazing that for a culture that spends billions of dollars annually on pain relief and need gratification, we have so little pleasure to show for it. Some Christians even have a negative slant on reliving their past hurt and pain. They believe it is a sign that they have not been forgiven or that they are still holding on to the old sinful nature that is within them. However, we have seen that if people are willing to look at their past hurt, they can allow God's grace to heal it and put it behind them.

Leading people into their journey through pain has brought us to the conclusion that pleasure is not the absence of pain, nor is it pain's antonym. Rather, pain is actually a part of pleasure's process, a crucible, if you will, that not only signals that there is a need in the soul but also helps the soul to bloom.

Feeling Is Healing

There is an old Alcoholics Anonymous slogan that states, "You can't heal what you can't feel." Defense mechanisms may help for a while, but eventually our bodies and our souls will remind us of our repressed pain, in a way repaying us for not feeling it the first time.

Like many other adult children of abuse, I had tried all kinds of ways to defend against feeling my childhood pain. I made excuses for my parents. I saw the "silver lining" in the dark clouds. I got busy trying to heal others. I read books about healing the dysfunctional family. I went to classes and attended seminars on inner healing. I did anything but *feel* the pain. All the while, my body kept score with depression, headaches, stomach problems, and fatigue.

I was not alone in my ignorance; many people's physical illnesses have their roots in unresolved soul pain. These are called psychosomatic disorders. Even though so many people suffer from these types of maladies, most of them, like me, would rather wrestle a shark, or take their chances with Daniel in the lion's den, than feel all the pain of the past. Yet, it is the only way to be truly healed.

Sandra's Journey Through Pain

This was the journey we encouraged Sandra, and many other clients, to take. She had a difficult time at first, dealing with her painful past. Her "why" questions haunted her. She was constantly asking God why things had to happen the way they did in her life. Her answers were found in the school of pain. With pain as her mentor, she began to piece together the puzzle of her past hurts. She eventually saw God's healing hand in the formation of her inner strength. She learned from the past and from her relationship struggles, rather than pushing away from them. By revealing and experiencing the effects of her childhood wounds, Sandra gained wisdom and insight that began to free her soul. Pain led her on a healing journey. And that journey began in her family of origin.

Family of Origin

Family of origin is the therapeutic term for the family we were raised in. This terminology is used in contrast to the term *nuclear family*, which is the family with whom we now live. To be more specific, our family of origin includes our parents, grandparents, and siblings, while our nuclear family includes us, our spouse, and our children.

Our family of origin provides us with much information about our childhood wounds. Our past tells us about who we are and why we do what we do in relationships. Most of our interactions with people were learned in our families of origin. For example, if we grew up in an emotionally abusive home, we may have a tendency to abuse others or to be emotionally abused in our present relationships. Dr. Patricia Love, a well-known marital therapist and author, makes a startling statement in her seminars that "to the extent we have been abused in childhood, we can be abused or abuse."[1] Patterns of dysfunction may continue, unless we are willing to become aware of their effects.

There are two other critical issues applied to relationships that are also learned in family of origin: self-esteem and security. *Self-esteem* is learned through the relationships children have *individually* with their mother and father. If those relationships are healthy, then children will grow up feeling good about themselves. If those relationships are laden with abuse, neglect, and criticism, the child's self-esteem will suffer. *Security*, on the other hand, is learned as children observe their mother and father's relationship with each other. If that relationship is healthy and loving, children will grow to feel a sense of security about love and relationships. If that marriage is full of conflict, discord, and strife, then the child will grow up suspicious of relationships, and will feel insecure in them, especially in love relationships.

Types of Childhood Abuse

Dr. David Seamands in his book, *Healing Damaged Emotions*, writes about the types of family systems that may leave scars on individuals and cause them problems as adults. He qualifies abuse in two categories: active and passive. *Active abuse* connotes overt physical, verbal, and sexual abuse. Some examples of this may be beating, hitting, slapping, name calling, threatening, blaming, and shaming. My mother often made the statement that if abortion were legal, she would have gotten rid of me. This overt verbal abuse created a deep scar on my soul that stayed with me even as an adult. Examples of active sexual abuse are fondling, molestation, and intercourse, initiated by a parent or adult toward a child.

Passive abuse is more subtle or covert. This type of abuse is more in the emotional or psychological area. Examples of this include not being told you were loved, not being hugged or physically nurtured, being subtly criticized for not being as good, pretty, or athletic as a sibling. Never feeling as if your parents were there for you is a form of passive abuse. Many of the "boomer" generation grew up with fathers who worked long hours and spent a great deal of time away from home. Because of this, their children may carry a deep feeling of neglect or abandonment. If you grew up with a perfectionist mother who was constantly critical, you could be a victim of passive emotional abuse. If you grew up in a home with parents who did not love each other or who were in constant conflict, you may carry psychological or emotional scars.

More detailed examples of active abuse include:

- physical — hitting, slapping, beating
- verbal — name calling, threatening
- emotional — using fear and violence as a motivator
- sexual — fondling, molestation, intercourse

Passive abuse often involves the following:

- physical — being neglected or abandoned; being left alone too often
- verbal — being told you were not wanted or loved
- emotional — overprotection, spoiling, emotional incest; being told that you were bad, or being falsely blamed or shamed
- sexual — demeaning sexual slurs; being leered at while undressing or bathing

All of these abuses can leave scars in a person's psyche. They can also be the seed bed in which relational trouble grows. Many of the adults we treat in our counseling center can trace their marital trouble back to childhood.

Cindy's Story

Cindy, a young college student, came to our counseling center because she was having panic attacks. She told me that her parents did not love each other and had stayed together for the sake of the children. As her therapy progressed, I was able to trace her anxiety disorder to a fear of growing up and having a marriage just like her parents. Even though her parents were trying to help her by staying unhappily married all those years, this was passively abusive to Cindy. She became very insecure because of the lack of love she experienced in her family. She developed an inner belief that all relationships would turn out badly. This caused her to be very anxious about life, which fostered her panic disorder. I read a slogan many years ago that said: *The greatest gift a father can give to his children is to love their mother.* Cindy and her parents could have benefited from heeding this advice.

Overprotection and overindulgence are two other forms of passive abuse. Spoiled children can become narcissistic adults who feel entitled and who have unhealthy expectations in their adult relationships.

Examples of passive sexual abuse are: being watched as you undress or bathe, inappropriate displays of parental nudity, obscene statements or gestures made by family members, or being made to look at indecent sexual material (Farmer 18–84).

Emotional incest is a form of passive sexual abuse. This is when one parent puts all of their love and energy into their child rather than into their mate. Although there is no active sexual abuse, the child is made to play the role of the husband or wife in the family. This creates a very unhealthy enmeshment between parent and child. The child grows up feeling that love is suffocating, confining, and demanding. Boys who were emotionally incested by their mothers may have poor or estranged relationships with their fathers.

Their unhealthy bonding with mom not only makes dad feel left out, but it also sets up an unhealthy sense of competition between father and son for mom's affection and attention. Many men who have been emotionally incested fear commitment. These men have said in therapy that they have a fear that if they marry, they will somehow betray their mother (Love 51ff).

If you think you may have suffered from active or passive abuse, here are some symptoms that are characteristic of these victims (Seamands 30–45):

- supersensitivity
- perfectionism
- low self-esteem
- sense of unworthiness
- wrong idea of God
- fear of failure
- depression
- fear of commitment
- fear of rejection
- lack of trust in self and others
- active addictions, both negative and positive
- lack of forgiveness
- critical spirit
- bitterness and resentment

Although many of these characteristics can come naturally as part of our human nature, or as a result of innate temperament, if you are having trouble in these areas it is worth exploring your childhood to see if any roots exist.

It is often hard to look at our parents as perpetrators. Even if we grew up in blatantly dysfunctional homes, where there was violence, alcoholism, incest, or mental illness, there is still a tendency to deny that our parents had any fault. We want to preserve their sacred image and believe that they were like a "Leave-It-to-Beaver" family. In some ways this makes us feel as if we are all right as well.

Ivan Boze-MeniNage, a famous French family therapist, once said, "Your parents are still your parents, whether they are a thousand miles away, or dead and buried. They have placed an indelible mark on your souls that transcends time. Your emphatic 'No' only proves the power of their transgenerational strings that tie your souls together" (187ff).

Rather than deny the existence of soul wounds, we invite you to go on a journey of soul exploration. The goal here is not to assign blame but rather to find out the truth. The Scripture says, "You shall know the truth and the truth shall set you free" (Jn 8:32). Finding the truth about our childhood wounds allows us to look honestly at our adult relationship patterns and begin to heal them. Healing is our goal, not blame.

Blame Is Not Our Game

One of the biggest hurdles we must jump as we begin to examine our family of origin is that of accusing or blaming our parents for our current relationship struggles and, conversely, of not taking personal responsibility for our actions. In understanding family-of-origin issues therapeutically, we are doing neither. The objective is to understand our childhood programming, with mother and father as the primary teachers who taught us based upon their own possibly faulty learning. We do this without casting any blame or condemnation on them. They were, after all, only living out their own family-of-origin programming.

We are also not advocating a lack of personal responsibility for our own actions. Understanding where and how we learned to behave in relationships is our primary goal. When an individual can trace the inception of certain dysfunctional behaviors, he or she can then take responsibility for accepting and changing certain actions. We must be willing to examine our behaviors objectively, without denial or blame. Evaluating our childhood and the behavior patterns we learned there with honesty, openness, and forgiveness can give us a great deal of freedom and spontaneity in our adult relationships. We will become less likely to repeat our parents' dysfunctional behaviors and thus become more likely to pass on healthy relationship skills to the next generation.

Mike and Carol's Story

Mike and Carol were great examples of people who had not dealt with the issues in their families of origin. Carol came into our office because her marriage was in trouble. She suspected Mike was having an affair. She had no concrete proof, but all the signs were there. Among other things, they were not having sex. Mike generally traveled all week and spent the majority of his weekends on the golf course. Since the youngest of their three daughters had gone off to college, Carol had become very lonely. She began to actively seek out Mike's company, but found him to be detached, cool, and unavailable. Carol sensed that Mike had started drifting away from her about ten years earlier, but like many wives, she ignored that which was too painful to deal with and threw herself into raising her children. Now that the kids were grown, Carol had to do some serious soul searching. What had happened to her relationship with Mike? Had they both drifted away? Could they recover their passion and love for each other? Did each really want to? In answering these questions, Carol soon came upon some painful realizations.

She confronted Mike with her suspicions and was met with the usual anger and vehement denial. She begged him to come to therapy, but he would have no part of it. She finally talked him into attending one of our Soul Healers Workshops. Reluctantly, Mike came and sat there listening to the theories of childhood pain in family of origin, and how this pain subsequently affects people in adult relationships today. Mike was squirming in his chair, and it was obvious that he was uncomfortable with the topic. Finally, he spoke up, "I can hardly remember my childhood at all, and I sure don't have any so-called childhood pain! Besides, what could this possibly have to do with how I behave today? That stuff happened forty years ago."

It was hard to believe, with all the material written about self-help and inner healing and with all the television talk shows in the last fifteen years, that Mike had no awareness of this kind of pain. But he didn't; rather, he wouldn't entertain this idea. We gently, yet determinedly, helped him begin to open up to an awareness of his childhood issues. We suggested that he had probably repressed a good portion of his early memories because they were too painful to remember. Oftentimes we see people with particularly burdensome childhoods who repress more than normal because their pain is just too much to bear. Mike's repression of his childhood exemplified this. Slowly, but surely, he began to deal with these issues. He poured out stories about his prostitute mother and a father he had never known. His mother was very aloof and distant, and Mike did not feel wanted by her. When he was six years old, his mother was sent to prison, and he was placed in the home of his elderly paternal grandparents. Several years later his grandmother passed away, leaving him with a cold and critical grandfather. At age sixteen, he left home and joined the military. He had been in some type of military service ever since. Mike was now at the rank of colonel and was serving in the Army Reserves. He felt that the military had given him the structure and sense of belonging that he had never had in his life. In the military he was important and significant; in the military he was part of a "family," no longer an orphan who did not belong. This met a very deep emotional need for Mike, but the negative aspect was that he could relate to other people only as a colonel. He related to his wife and children in a harsh, military fashion.

Carol was raised in a Christian home and said that her parents loved her, but they always compared her to her beautiful and talented older sister. This made Carol feel as if she was not good enough, so she tried hard to win the approval of others. When Mike related to her in a severe fashion, this impacted her inadequacy wound. Once again we see the principle of interactivity played out in relationships. Mike's wounds caused him to relate to Carol in a way that impacted her wounds. Carol would withdraw from Mike, which reminded him of his cold, withdrawn grandfather. Being a husband and father was very difficult for Mike, because he had had so little modeling of how a family was supposed to interact, let alone really love one another. His family-of-origin experience left him sorely lacking in relationship skills and deeply wounded.

One day in our office as Mike was opening up to his painful past, he began to weep for the first time since his grandmother had died so many years before. Carol held him, as he began to recount forgotten memories of a lost childhood filled with pain. He realized that he had been forever looking for a soft, loving mother figure only to become distant and aloof once he found her. In this way, he was reliving his fear of abandonment. These insights gave Mike tremendous awareness about his current behavior patterns with his family. Both Mike and Carol agreed that had Mike not had the courage and determination to explore the pain of his family of origin, their marriage would have ended.

They were richly blessed because they continued to work faithfully toward discovering the relationship they had never experienced. Mike gave up the affair he had been having. Carol worked very hard to forgive him. They both labored diligently to establish a deep soul-healing love they had never before thought possible. Mike and Carol were one couple who took our advice and decided to face their painful past together, so they could heal their wounds. Their work paid off, giving them the love they had always wanted.

Unfortunately, other couples do not choose this option. Some people remain as Mike started out, claiming that they had no such pain in childhood. While there are certainly some families out there who can claim this truth, our overwhelming experience has been that most families will have lived and behaved in some way (even if it was in accord with the social mores of the time) that impacted their children negatively. Most people will have experienced some kind of pain in childhood. Many will have scars. If this is so, then they must be willing to examine their past, deal with the wounds, and heal that pain. At this point they are ready to learn to become soul healers.

As you can probably see, by asking yourself some painfully honest questions about your childhood upbringing, you can begin to gather valuable information about past and present relationship patterns. Virtually all of the conscious and unconscious information about these patterns is stored within the soul. It is as if there is a tiny diskette deep inside the soul that contains volumes of information about how a person experiences life, love, and relationships, both past and present. Accessing the information will greatly aid you in unlearning negative patterns and relearning new and healthy behaviors. In this chapter you learned that feeling your pain puts you on the path of soul healing. The next chapter shows you how to attend to your soul in the healing process.

Chapter 4

Attending the Soul

In the previous chapters we learned that the soul is defined as our essence or being, the guts of our psyche. We also learned that these guts contain the wounds of childhood, family of origin, past relationships, culture, and society. In our souls lie the conscious and unconscious information about how we view men, women, religion, life, marriage, God, and countless other issues. It is a database that has been collecting information for a lifetime. Often, we are not consciously aware that this information even exists until our views become challenged in some way.

This chapter is going to show you how to access this important information in order to become aware of what is buried deep within your soul. This exercise will teach you a great deal about your current belief systems and relationship patterns. In this chapter, you are going to learn how to attend to your soul.

Peter's Soul Impressions

Peter came into our counseling center because he was forty-three years old and had never been married. Although he had dated many women, whenever the relationship progressed to the point of real closeness or commitment, he would find a reason to break up.

"Peter," I asked, " what is your impression or idea of women?"

"What?" he replied, almost offended. "What do you mean, what do I think of women? I love women! I think about women all the time. I want to be married. Why do you think I date so much?"

I responded by saying that when we see a relationship pattern such as Peter's (of dating many women up to the point of commitment and then abruptly ending the relationship), it often means that there must be deeper issues than just not finding the right woman. Usually these issues have to do with the man's impressions of women locked deep within the soul.

As Peter continued in therapy, he began to look at the guts of his psyche, and he soon discovered that he had an unconscious idea or notion of women that was not so positive. This started with his feelings about his own mother. Although he loved his mother very much, and described her as good and loving, he also realized that she was controlling and somewhat suffocating. He was a pleaser and never wanted to disappoint her. This further aggravated his sense of suffocation, because he felt guilty if he was different from what she would prefer. Peter realized that unconsciously he believed that all women would control and oppress him, and thus he feared intimacy and bailed out of the relationship when things got too close. Tom and I call Peter's obscured feeling and sensation about women a *soul impression*. This is a feeling or impression that exists even when there is little foundation for it. If you have a very deep impression in your soul that marriage ends in destruction, or that all men are users, yet there is little conscious information, family history, or life experience to validate it, you may have a soul impression. Many people come into counseling with negative sensations or soul impressions that have left deep scars on their souls.

Soul Impressions

Soul impressions are different from cognitions because they are not only known, they are also sensed and felt. These impressions are sentient, characterized by a sensation and consciousness that is oftentimes felt in the soul first and then throughout the senses. Songs and movies that override the logical, rational left brain and move to the more feeling, sensing right brain can also create soul impressions. Have you ever heard the words or melody of a certain song that sweeps your soul away to a blissful place, and then many years later when you hear the same song, you are instantly swept away with the same rapture? That song may have left a soul impression.

These impressions also involve the intuitive, mystical quality of our mind, body, and will that have no logical or rational explanation. Religious experiences can create soul impressions. While these types of experiences can affect the conscious mind, they can also leave their mark on the soul. Many times when we have these types of experiences, we know that something is different in our lives; our senses, feelings, and will are also affected. Soul impressions of a religious nature touch us in a very deep and spiritual way.

Negative and positive childhood experiences can leave soul impressions, just as they did in Peter's case. You may have an intuitive feeling about someone or something based on past occurrences, and yet have no cognitive proof, or rational validation for this feeling or sensation. This is a soul impression.

Soul Impressions and Relationships

People can enter and leave relationships based on their soul impressions. Many people fall in love based on data from positive soul impressions. Couples may find that they have identical soul impressions that help them form a lasting bond. Identifying similar soul impressions can help dating couples find prospective marriage partners.

An example of this is evident in our own courtship. While Tom and I were dating we discussed our faith. He and I had very similar ideas about religion. I was pleased with our conversations because spiritual compatibility in marriage was very important to me. One day Tom asked me to share my favorite hymn. As I began to ponder this, he started quietly singing the words to "His Eye Is on the Sparrow"—my favorite hymn. I was singing the words in my head at the very same time. This created a bond between Tom and me. My soul impression confirmed that he was a good and safe person for me to love.

Examining the Soul's Data

To better understand how soul impressions impact our love relationships, we must examine more closely the soul's data that has been collected regarding love. Once again let's look at the relationship between Tom and me. I grew up seeing love as difficult, violent, and ending in tragedy. Cognitively, I learned from Scripture and other material that love was good and right and true, but my soul impression was very negative. Because of this, the notion of marriage created a great deal of anxiety for me. Tom was raised in the church, so he had heard sermons and lectures about the wonders of love between lifetime partners. However, he grew up watching his parents struggle in their marriage and finally divorce, which created a very negative soul impression within him. Now, take these two hopeful romantics, with all of their knowledge, training, and education on healthy relationships, and you would think you could get two successful soul-healing lovers. Unfortunately, this was not the case. Our negative soul impressions reared their ugly heads and wreaked havoc on our positive cognitions of love and marriage. Our soul impressions won out over our rational knowledge of love, and this left us feeling anxious and fearful.

Love Begets Fear and Panic

When an individual is in doubt, panic, or crisis, soul impressions will win over cognitive knowledge every time. When you are in a state of anxiety, most often your gut will win over your head. Therefore, no matter how many books you read, seminars you attend, or sermons you sit through, you still have to battle your negative soul impressions. They effectively counteract all of your positive information and training on love. It is no wonder adult children of pain and dysfunction have so much trouble with matrimony.

Recognizing this dilemma, Tom and I decided to set out on a journey to relearn or readjust negative soul impressions toward a much more positive view of love. To do this, we first had to examine how the human brain works in collecting soul data.

The Old Brain and the New Brain

In Robert Ornstein and David Sobel's book *The Healing Brain*, we learn how the brain aids in compiling information within our souls. The human brain is divided into two basic parts: the cerebral cortex and the brain stem. The cerebral cortex is the highly functioning part of the brain that is only present in humans. It helps us take in information, organize it, and make decisions.

This *new brain*, as many refer to it, gives us the ability to observe ourselves and evaluate our own behavior. The difference between humans and animals is that humans can objectively critique and assess what we do. I can't picture my dog barking frantically at the paper boy and then thinking, "I'll bet I really looked stupid doing that." Sometimes when we do something really embarrassing such as "losing it" in the grocery store because the checker is too slow, the gift of seeing ourselves in our mind's eye may not seem so wonderful after all, but we have the ability to do just that.

Beneath the new brain lies the brain stem. Cradled at the root of the brain stem is the limbic system, the seat of very powerful emotions. It is our self-defense reflex, or our survival mechanism. This instinctual *old brain* is aware of reality only through sensations and feelings. Since its main function is survival, the old brain recognizes certain patterns it has learned to associate with fear, danger, loss, and death. It is unable to make decisions like the new brain, so it draws all its conclusions from circumstances and often overreacts in a quick-fire fashion to certain stimuli. For example, you are driving down the road on a rainy day and the road is slippery. Suddenly, you see that the cars ahead of you have stopped. You instinctively slam on your brakes. Your heart is beating fast, and your palms are sweaty. Your old brain's survival instinct is operating full-force.

It is important to know that the limbic system or old brain is not conscious of time. It is atemporal, which means that something recorded in the system at age five can be felt again at age thirty-five with the same fear, danger, and risk as before (Hendrix, *Keeping* 41). I had a client who as a child had burned her hand on a pot-bellied stove. This was quite frightening to her because her parents were out drinking, and there was no one there to care for her. To this day she has a serious aversion to these stoves and will not even allow her husband to buy a wood-burning stove for their home. Her irrational, deep-seated feelings about stoves are what Tom and I call an "old brainer" or a "limbic." It is obvious to most of us that wood-burning stoves are not dangerous, but my client is not using her rational thought processes. Her interminable limbic system has been kicked into overdrive. Thus, an "old brainer" has occurred.

The Old Brain and Relationships

As we have seen, many of us can have problems in the present that have their roots in past trauma. Although "old brainers" may not seem so serious when it comes to pot-bellied stoves or slippery highways, having such negative feelings and sensations about love can be perilous.

In my own life, love was recorded in my limbic system as dangerous, even deadly. To me, love meant pain, abuse, and abandonment. My old brain aided in my very negative soul impression of love. Let me share a personal example with you.

When I was a young girl, I would listen to my parents fight, and I would become anxious and fearful because the conflicts would result in violence, and my father would leave. He would often stay gone for several days. I couldn't really blame him (I would have gone too if I could), but I was still left with a very angry, violent mother. Many times I feared for my own and my siblings' safety.

Years later, as a budding bride of two months, I was sitting at the kitchen table with my young husband discussing quiche, of all things. He hated it, and I was forcefully arguing with him about its many virtues. Unable to convince me of his distaste for mushy egg dishes, he suddenly said, "I'm leaving. I'm gonna go out on the porch and cool off."

When he was young, his mother told him that all good, hot-blooded Portuguese boys should cool off when they got angry. His mother taught him, in lieu of losing his temper, to go outside and calm down. One would think that I, his bride, would see the healthy rationale in this—but no! I had a major "old brainer."

"Leave! Did I hear you say leave?" The danger bell rang in the limbic factory and there I was—anxious, panicked, full of the fear of death. I clung. I cried. I grabbed his leg. "Please don't leave. How could you be so mean as to leave me at a time like this?!"

"Huh?" he sighed incredulously. "What are you so upset about? I'm just cooling off like my mom taught me years ago! Can't a guy get a break around here?"

My limbic system did not want to give Tom a break. My old brain and negative soul impressions told me that when a man leaves, he may not come back. At that point, I was not thinking like a young, sensible bride. I was thinking like an abandoned little girl.

It was very difficult for Tom and me that night. Needless to say, our honeymoon haven had been disrupted by one of the many "old brainers" that we were yet to learn about in our marriage.

"Old Brainers" and Marital Strife

Knowing what we know about the power of "old brainers" to bring destruction to couples, it is easy to see how these experiences, along with negative soul impressions, can be activated in the course of a couple's sharing simple information with each other. We often see that one partner becomes fearful, angry, and overemotional and draws false conclusions about the other partner who then also becomes angry and fearful and hurls a few false conclusions or accusations as well. Dr. Patricia Love calls this "making up your own reality about your partner."[1]

As you can see, I had made up my own reality that Tom would leave me. I drew a false conclusion that he would do as other men had done in my past. And, this is where it gets tricky, because I then accused him of something he did not, or would not, do. My indictment could have been so hurtful that he *would* leave, and thus I would have created the reality that I feared so greatly. He did not leave, but my false assumption did activate an "old brainer" in him. He started feeling suffocated and "clung-to" just as he had in his relationship with his mother. He reacted to this, and it caused World War III in our marriage. Our wounds were indeed interactive and our statements became impact statements. Both of our responses to our own woundedness served to hurt each other. We felt like the Apostle Paul in Romans, when he said, "I do not understand what I do. For what I want to do I do not do, but what I hate I do" (7:15). One of my greatest fears was that Tom would leave me, yet my hysterics could actually have facilitated this reality. My "old brainer" could have actually made it hard for him to stay. I was doing that which I hated, because I was responding out of my fear and creating a struggle for my husband. We see this kind of interactivity in our own marriage, and as therapists, we see it with couples every day. Because of these false accusations, negative soul impressions, and "old brainers," painful impact statements are made, and then the couple must spend a great deal of time cleaning up their relational messes.

Family Ghosts and Negative Soul Impressions

Making up our own reality about our partner is similar to what transgenerational therapists call the phenomenon of *family ghosts.* The theory is that the ghosts of our parents, siblings, and ex-partners show up in current relationships. Transgenerational therapists call it "putting someone else's face on your spouse." When I was fearful of Tom leaving me, I was "putting my father's abandoning face on him." Putting the faces of past "ghosts" on current relationships can lead to trouble. Take Ann Marie for example.

Ann Marie's Family Ghosts

Ann Marie came to the counseling center because she was struggling in her two-year relationship with Donald. There were times she felt a great deal of love for Donald, but at other times, her feelings would shift so quickly that she would break the relationship off in a panic. Later she would come to her senses and reunite with him. She came to counseling to determine, once and for all, if Don was the one for her, and to see if they could make it as a successful married couple.

When I questioned her about her childhood, I found that she was the middle child of three girls. Her father, a local orthodontist, was a very critical man and seemed to feel responsible for straightening out his daughters' lives as well as their teeth. Dad constantly criticized Ann Marie and her sisters and belittled them in public. Whenever she would bring home her report card, Dad would first notice what was lacking, "Ann Marie, what is this A-minus in Latin? You should be able to make an A-plus." As a result, Ann Marie never felt that she measured up to her dad, or in any of her relationships for that matter.

After further questioning about her relationship with Donald, Ann Marie told me that he also was very critical. She shared with me several instances in which he told her what spice to use in the chili, or that she had a dry spot on her nose so perhaps she should put some lotion on it. I could not say with absolute certainty that Don was well meaning in his motives, but these statements did not seem to be critical, as much as merely helpful comments. Ann Marie was so sensitive to measuring up that she was putting her father's face on Donald when he offered simple advice.

Once Ann Marie began to understand this behavior, she became free to see Donald for who he really was. As her soul started to heal, and the "ghosts" of the past were exorcised, she was free to love and to be loved. She and Donald could then start on their journey to become soul-healing partners.

Reactivity

The definition of *reactivity* is to use more emotion in a situation than it deserves. As we stated earlier, many painful memories of our past are stored in the old brain. These memories can be triggered and activated by stimuli in our present relationships. Let's say that your mother was very lax in preparing food for you as a child. Let's also assume that your wife forgot to pack your lunch as you were leaving for work. You may have one of many responses. You may tell her that you are disappointed and ask that she do better in the future. You may also just overlook it and decide to eat out with your associates. But if you overreact, get enraged, yell, threaten, accuse, or pout, then you are being reactive. When you are giving the situation more attention, emotion, or anger than it deserves, you are in a state of reactivity. It is almost a sure bet that if you are being reactive, a childhood wound is being activated.

Ann Marie was being reactive when she felt Donald was criticizing her. Her reactivity caused her to withdraw from him, and this created some reactivity for Donald as well. It is common for a couple's reactivity to be interactive; that is, what affects her will also wound him, and vice versa. Reactivity can create many problems in relationships. Just ask Ann Marie and Donald, and they will tell you that reactivity was one of their greatest barriers to having a healthy relationship.

In becoming a soul healer, we learn to control our reactivity and give the situation only the emotion it deserves. We learn to recognize our past wounds, allow God to heal them, and therefore, deal with what triggers our reactivity so we will learn to have appropriate reactions in all of our relationships.

Accessing Information in the Soul

From Ann Marie's example, we learn that it is not easy for people to get in touch with painful feelings from their childhood. Humans can have very well honed defense mechanisms that prevent them from feeling their pain. Many times we, as therapists, must help people override those defenses by other means. Tom and I designed a tool to override our defense mechanisms and to allow the Holy Spirit to show us information and patterns that occur within our souls. This tool uses our cognitive and subliminal resources to aid in soul reflection. The tool is called the Soul Healogram. Here is how it works.

EXERCISE 1: THE SOUL HEALOGRAM

Give yourself forty-five minutes to complete this exercise. Find a quiet place. Pray and ask the Lord to guide you in accessing your unconscious memories. In my healing, I have found him to be a great soul tour guide. Because the space in the book is limited, you may wish to get a much larger piece of paper to do this exercise, and use the outline on page 65 as a guideline. Or enlarge the outline on a copy machine.

On your paper you will see a large box that represents you; beside it is a box that represents your spouse, if you are married. The box just above your box represent your parents. Above them are boxes representing your grandparents on both your mother's and father's side. The small boxes beside your own represent your siblings. The small boxes beside your parents represent your paternal and maternal aunts and uncles. If any cousins played a significant role in your life, draw a small box for them as well.

From this diagram you will see a transgenerational panorama of your family of origin and descendants. To many of you, the drawing may look some what like a genogram, a tool used in social work and family therapy. Write the names of each person above each box. You will see a line in the center of each box. In the top half of each box, write the *negative* characteristics of these family members. In the bottom half, write the *positive* characteristics.

Out to the side of each box, list any soul impressions you have of these people. Remember soul impressions are sensations and perceptions, not necessarily actual realities. You need not have known these family members personally or spent any time with them to have definite soul impressions about them. Make sure you write the letters *SI* beside each soul impression.

Label and fill in boxes for as many generations as you have information. It is best if you can fill in at least three generations because you will be able to see some patterns repeating themselves in your family.

If you do not remember a family member, you may write down what you have heard about him or her from family folklore. For example, I never knew my maternal grandmother, but I've heard from various family members that she was worrisome and very passive. She was married to my grandfather, a very violent, cruel alcoholic who abused her regularly. I was told that when she was pregnant with my mother, my grandfather went on a drinking binge and did not come home for weeks. My grandmother had no income, so she began to beg for food for herself and her children. The townspeople took pity on her and put their leftover cornbread, beans, and fatback out on the lids of their garbage pails, so when she came by she would have food to eat. I was told that my grandmother constantly worried about money and was always concerned about where her next meal was coming from. Learning this information from family folklore gave me tremendous insight into my family and myself.

As long as I can remember, my mother had an inordinate fear of poverty. She constantly feared that she was going to be penniless, even if there was no good reason to feel this way. What amazed me was that as far back as I could trace, I also had a deep-seated fear that I was not going to have enough money to make ends meet. Many times there was no logical rationale for this fear. In learning about my grandmother, I realized that many of her fears were passed down to my mother and me, yet there was no reasonable explanation for us to entertain them.

These "curses" can be passed down generationally, much like diseases and other hereditary conditions. It says in Exodus, "I the Lord your God will visit the iniquity of the fathers upon the children to the third and fourth generations of those who hate Me, but showing mercy to thousands, to those who love Me and keep my commandments" (20:5–6). Apparently, these curses or patterns had been visited on my family for three generations.

As you complete this exercise, you may see these unexplainable patterns or curses within your own family. This insight can
be very beneficial for the healing of your soul.

Take some time now and complete the Soul Healogram.

The Soul Healogram

Draw your family tree as far back as you can remember. Write the names of each person at the top of each box. List the negative characteristics at the top of the boxes, and the positive characteristics at the bottom. List all soul impressions beside each box.

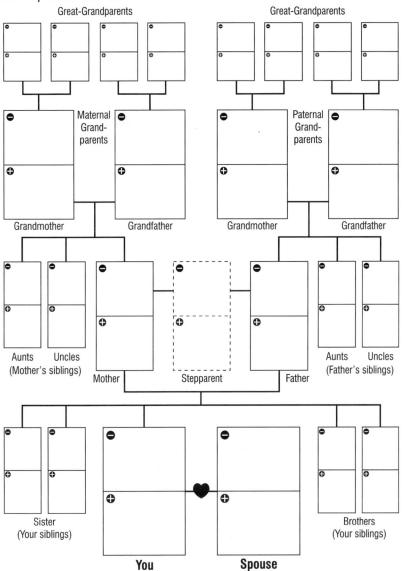

From *Soul-Healing Love* by Beverly and Tom Rodgers ©1998 Resource Publications, Inc.

The Soul Healogram can point out insightful information about repetitive family patterns. This tool can also show you reasons for certain behaviors that you could not logically explain.

As you complete the Soul Healogram, take a yellow highlighter and find all the similarities you can see in the positive and negative characteristics of your family members. Record them on a separate list at the bottom of the page. Do the same for the soul impressions for each family member. As you do this, you will see common characteristics or themes develop. When you have finished, complete the following:

From my Soul Healogram, I have learned that:

Men in my family are _____

_____

Women in my family are _____

_____

Marriage in my family is _____

_____

Conflict in my family is _____

_____

Communication in my family is _____

_____

Coping in my family is _____

_____

Feelings in my family are _____

_____

The addictive patterns in my family are _____

_____

In my family, divorce is _____

_____

In my family, abuse is _____

_____

In my family, God is _____

_____

In my family, religion is _____

_____

Based on the data I have collected, I have an inner belief that my marriage is [will be] _____

_____

and that my mate is [will be] _____

_____

As I learn to heal the wounds within me from my family and society, I would like my idea of marriage to be _____

_____

_____

I can be reactive about the following issues _____

_____

_____

These are the wounds I would like to heal _____

_____

_____

These are the patterns I would like to change _____

_____

_____

The following are the goals I will set for my own soul healing and healing the soul of my marriage...

1. _____

_____

2. _____

_____

3. _____

_____

4. _____

_____

5. _____

_____

Now that you have accessed some very important data from your unconscious, you are ready to begin the soul-healing process. The next chapter is dedicated to how this process can happen.

Chapter 5

The Soul in Healing

N ow that you have completed the Soul Healogram in the previous chapter, you may be surprised at what is buried deep within your unconscious mind. Since you're now able to see a cross section of your unconscious, you can bring these insights to the forefront of your conscious mind. There are many realizations that you will make after reviewing the data on your Soul Healogram. For example, you may see that a lot of the men in your family were critical and controlling. As a result, you may have a tendency to overinterpret your spouse's behavior as critical or controlling, when this may only be partially true. It may seem to you that most of the women in your family were passive enablers. Because of this, you may become too passive in your marriage, or you may compensate by being too controlling.

As you gain these types of insights into your soul, it is important to set goals that move you and your mate toward healing. The best way to do this is to write these goals down. We encourage couples to sit down together and write what we call a *Soul-Healing Plan*.

EXERCISE 2A: THE SOUL-HEALING PLAN — INDIVIDUAL SOUL-HEALING GOALS

This plan will include individual goals as well as goals for your relationship. Each goal should be dated and given a feasible completion date. Start with individual goals first. This is important because many people come into counseling with no idea of how to nurture their own soul. They in turn project their lack of happiness onto their spouse, which can cause them a great deal of marital strife. They blame their partners for the emptiness within their souls.

Over the years, we have put together a list of ways that have been soul healing for Tom and me, and also helpful for many people we have treated in counseling. We would like to share some of these soul-healing experiences with you.

One of the ways to heal your soul is to begin to listen to it and to pay attention to what it is trying to tell you. The concept of listening to the soul is discussed in great detail in Thomas Moore's *Care of the Soul.* Moore makes a wonderfully strong case for slowing down and attending to the soul (19ff). The following sampling of soul-healing activities may be included in your Soul-Healing Plan.

Soul healing through meditation and prayer. There are many pathways to listening to the soul. Prayer and meditation are two significant ways. Through them we can listen to ourselves, and we can also hear from God. There are times when I have been silent before God and he begins to tell me what my soul needs are before I even realize it. Silence can be a very good way to attend to the soul. I have a friend who facilitates silent retreats where no one speaks for the entire weekend. Many participants report astounding spiritual renewal. Some even say they hear the voice of God for the very first time.

Soul healing through therapy. Therapy can be a wonderful way to care for the soul. Tom and I haven't always been people helpers. Once we sat at the feet of great soul healers. We, too, were clients of therapy. I am grateful for the many hours that I spent with healers as I poured out stories of painful scenes from my childhood. Their merciful Christlike guidance showed me the way to heal my soul. It was the love of spiritual leaders and mentors, as well as the mercy and insight of unconditionally loving therapists, that began to transform my soul and create a positive vision of love in my life.

Soul healing through mother earth. Eastern philosophy encourages us to get in touch with the earth, ground, water, and air to develop our more feminine side. To borrow their term we must find the yen of life. This is one way to "mother" the soul. This can come in very handy if you do not have a healthy female parent. Mothers are supposed to be good for soul nurturing, but they are often blocked from this. If this is the case with your mother, it may be hard for you to think of maternal things that you can do to heal your soul. I had this problem, and here is how I began to resolve it.

I have always been a busy person. In graduate school I would run from place to place in a flurry, often not noticing whether it was sunny or rainy. Certainly, I never noticed the flowers or the trees. I thought I did not have time for nature or God's creation. I had places to go, papers to write, and people to help. As I grew older and became more aware of my soul needs, I found a very special place in my life for nature. I have even taken up gardening. Never would I have thought that I would like to dig in the dirt like a happy carefree child, but it is one of the most fulfilling, soul-nurturing activities in my day. Sometimes I get so absorbed in my garden that I completely lose track of time. Often I come inside, covered with dirt from a long day in the garden. I am filthy and completely content. My soul feels happy and fed. Thomas Moore calls this feeling *soulfulness* (*Care* 24). I have a sign in my garden that says, "He who plants a garden works hand in hand with God." It is indeed true that the soul can be nourished as the soil is nourished.

Soul healing through worship. Worshiping God can be a wonderful experience in soul healing. Praise music offers a soul-connecting experience with our Creator. Worship reminds us that God is constantly in and through all of creation. It is our human response to God's ever-present love. Through praise and worship there can be a rapturous feeling of oneness between God and humankind, but worship can be difficult for some people.

As marital and family therapists, Tom and I have days when we hear the problems of today's families and our compassion for their pain often causes us to feel a deep burden. We call this a "soul weight." We have a saying on these days that "we have heard too much." You may have had these kinds of days, too. The times when your neighbor confides in you that she wants to leave her husband.

You hear from the prayer chain that an infant has cancer. Your child comes home with a story of betrayal from a trusted friend. These are the days when our souls need uplifting. In our home we put on praise music and allow it to minister to us and soothe our souls with God's love and presence.

Soul healing through laughter and play. Laughter is a great medicine for the soul. It is innate in children to laugh and play, but in many dysfunctional families, children are wounded in this area. In these homes laughter is discouraged, and seriousness is actively or passively rewarded. The natural playful instinct of children who grew up in these homes was robbed from them. They were wounded by statements like: "Stop showing off," "Don't act silly," "Don't make any noise." Laughter, seen as noisy and disruptive, was discouraged. These parents strongly shamed their children for laughing and playing. Some even punished them for it. This caused these children to split off from their natural state of playfulness. As adults, they became serious and stoic. This was the case in my home. Consequently I had to give myself permission to laugh and play. It took a while for me to feel comfortable doing this. Dr. Harville Hendrix says a good belly laugh can be a bonding experience for couples. He even adds this as a step in one of his communication techniques (*Getting* 185ff).

Hendrix is also a supporter of high-energy play for couples. This type of high-energy play creates a bonding and synergy between people that can be very fulfilling. Often we see couples who are in trouble, and they cannot remember the last time they played together. Some say they have even forgotten how to play with their partner. It has been said that couples who pray together, stay together. Now we add to this that couples who play together, also stay together. Tickle fights, wrestling matches, water gun matches, go-cart races, biking, volleyball, and soccer games are just a few of the activities couples and families can enjoy to raise their heart rate and their connectedness rate.

Soul healing through healing your inner child. There is a way to nurture the soul that many people have not thought about in years. Try to remember those things you did as a child that gave your soul wings. Thomas Moore says that a child is the face of soul, and to move against that would cause the soul to suffer (*Care* 53). Take a look at the ways you ignore and even shame your own childlikeness. Our society believes that people should be mature, strong, and grown-up. Any regression to childhood is strongly discouraged. Nevertheless, moving back to the ways of childhood can bring back the light-hearted spirit in many people. Go ahead, find the lost passions of your youth, and try them again. Ride a bike. Go on a hike. Play touch football with the whole family. Fly a kite. Build a model plane. Make a mess. It will feel good once you get used to it.

EXERCISE 2B: THE SOUL-HEALING PLAN — COUPLES' SOUL-HEALING GOALS

When you have assessed the needs of your soul and written some individual goals down on your Soul-Healing Plan, it is time to start looking at setting goals for your marriage. The Soul Healogram can be helpful in setting individual goals, but now we will focus our attention on how it helps couples develop a Soul-Healing Plan for their marriages.

Let's say that you learned from your Soul Healogram that there were more divorces in your family than stable long-term marriages. You may have an internal belief, or soul impression, that marriages do not last. Possible goals for your Soul-Healing Plan may read as follows:

Soul-Healing Plan

1-20-96 Find several couples who have healthy relationships and spend time with them, allowing them to mentor us. This will be done within the next 6 months.

1-20-96 Attend a Soul Healers Workshop within the next year.

1-22-96 Read one book on couple's communication together within the next 6 months.

As you can see, the goals are dated and given a completion time. This helps you and your spouse assess your progress, as well as stay motivated to accomplish your tasks. When you have completed your goals, plan a surprise or celebration to mark your accomplishment. This will add to your sense of achievement and encourage you to move even further ahead as a soul-healing couple. To help you better understand how to develop your own Soul-Healing Plan, we will walk you through how one particular couple developed goals from the information they collected from their Soul Healograms.

Donna's and Alex's Soul Healograms

Donna, a tall, thin, frenzied young woman, came into our office with Alex, her chubby, laid-back husband. After the birth of their third child, Donna noticed that their marriage had started suffering. Alex seemed to stay longer at his job as an insurance underwriter. Donna would complain and nag him to pay more attention to her and the children. He, in turn, would say he was working so much to make things better for their growing family.

Donna felt abandoned and alone, and Alex felt pressured and unappreciated. This is a very common marital struggle we see regularly in counseling: one mate wants closeness, and the other wants distance. Of course, they are attracted to each other. It is typical for individuals caught in such struggles to think that they have picked the wrong mate.

"I should just find a man who wants to spend time with his family," Donna said. We encouraged her to be patient and allow the Lord to bring healing through the therapeutic process. We also said that there was indeed hope for Alex and that we had treated many couples in their situation, with favorable outcomes. We told her that if she left Alex, there was a great possibility that she would not be attracted to a clinging male who seemed to want to spend all of his time with her. Opposites attract. There was a huge likelihood that she would be in the same boat with yet another partner, who had the same basic wounds and issues as Alex. We encouraged her to "dance with the one what brung ya," as my southern grandmother used to say. In other words, before you get off the dance floor or find another dance partner, stay with your original one and give the dance a chance. Donna and Alex started their dance by completing the Soul Healogram.

In her Soul Healogram, Donna saw that the women in her family, especially on her mom's side, were caretakers who seemed to be the glue that kept the families together. She noticed a pattern of aloof, distant men on her father's side, starting with her paternal grandfather and moving down the genetic line to her father, her uncle, and her brother. Almost all of the couples on both sides of her family appeared to have marriages she would describe as functional, but remote and detached. Donna never enjoyed family reunions because all of the married couples seemed so miserable. Early in life she started desiring to have a happy marriage and to be very different from the rest of her family. Donna had an interesting insight into her parents' marriage. Although nothing was ever said, she had a soul impression that her father was unfaithful to her mother. She concluded that the guilt of this undiscovered affair was one of the reasons her father stayed so distant from her mother. She had a fear that her own marriage would be like theirs. Because of these insights, she realized that she had placed very high expectations on her husband regarding how much time he spent with her and the children. She realized that she would become reactive if he became distant in any way. She shared this insight with Alex. Her brave and honest confession made Alex soften at her candor and lack of defensiveness.

Alex made his own realizations while completing his Soul Healogram. It was not surprising to us that he found the women in his family to be clingy, whiny, and very dependent. The men, on the other hand, were dominant, controlling, and distant. He saw that his own parents' marriage was a replica of his maternal grandparents, who were unhappily married for fifty-two years. The main thing he remembered about his grandparents' relationship was that they criticized each other constantly. He could see that his own parents were heading down that path. Alex saw women, especially his mother, as suffocating and needy. He admitted that he had a tendency to become reactive and to see Donna in this same light. We pointed out that he would be inclined to think that his wife was clingy, even when her request for closeness was legitimate. He could also put his mother's suffocating face on Donna and see her as another version of his mother. We tell couples that they will see their partner as they saw their caretakers because their unconscious eye is "trained" to do so.

Both Donna and Alex began to see the "catch-me-if-you-can" game they had been playing during their marriage. With Alex not wanting to be engulfed and Donna not wanting to be abandoned, they both played a part in keeping intimacy just out of reach. Both were dealing with reactivity and negative soul impressions that they projected onto each other. As Alex and Donna saw their patterns more clearly, they were able to set goals to improve their marriage. Here is how they did this.

Donna's and Alex's Soul-Healing Plan

Donna and Alex started by setting a goal to begin individual therapy to help deal with their family-of-origin patterns. Alex started counseling with Tom, and Donna came to see me. They did this right away. Another goal they set was to attend a Soul Healers Workshop within the next three months. With a little help from us, they set up date nights every other week which focused on having fun, talking, playing, and connecting. Alex agreed to give Donna a present of fifteen minutes at the end of every other day; she would share about her day, as he maintained eye contact, and focused attention solely on her. This did wonders for her need for closeness. Donna agreed to give Alex a present of lecture-free, nag-free evenings. When they did get their alone time, Donna would no longer complain, whine, beg, or lecture Alex on what he was not doing or on what needs he was not meeting. The game of "marital Pac-Man," or "catch-me-if you-can," began to cease as they started this process. Donna learned through therapy to make clear requests and to share her feelings and needs in a nonsuffocating fashion. By learning to openly ask for what she wanted without feeling guilty, Donna stopped whining and clinging to justify her needs to Alex. This made life for Alex more pleasant, and thus he wanted to meet her needs more often. The tension in their relationship began to subside, and things became more livable for both of them. So you can get a better idea of how to set soul-healing goals, we will show you a sampling of Donna's and Alex's Soul-Healing Plan.

Donna's and Alex's Soul-Healing Plan

1-25-96 Alex will start individual therapy with Tom.

1-20-96 Donna will start individual therapy with Bev .

We both will attend a Soul Healers Workshop within the next 3 months.

1-20 We will focus on learning communication techniques and use them once a week.

1-20-96 Alex will work on not withdrawing or shutting down while Donna is talking.

1-20-96 Donna will work on not lecturing, criticizing, or whining when discussing something with Alex.

1-22-96 We will have date nights every other week, preferably on Saturday. During the dates we will take turns picking fun things to do that will create bonding between us. Alex will start first.

We will share with each other any significant insights we gain from our individual therapy, as well as continue in marital therapy for 6 months.

As you can see, Donna's and Alex's marital therapy has gone beyond the typical deal-making, tit-for-tat, quid pro quo type of therapy that many receive. So often couples come into therapy with the goal of getting even or of rebalancing the power in the relationship. Many times as therapists, we feel like grade-school teachers with tattling children trying to get us to take sides, to scold their partner, or to make trades, rather than marriage counselors trying to heal the souls of couples. Donna and Alex moved beyond this "if-she-does-this-then-he'll-do-that" type of counseling. Their goal became to understand each other, to minister to each other, to give each other presents, and to agape each other with God's help. Their aim was to become soul healers.

One of the changes that Donna noticed first was that her tendency to judge Alex's motives harshly began to subside. After seeing him struggle and work through his Soul Healogram, she started to envision Alex as wounded and thus developed empathy for him where there once was criticism and control. This helped her stop clinging, controlling, and nagging and start calmly asking for what she needed. She began to get a clearer picture of who Alex was without all of her added projections and reactivity.

The insight and help Donna received from her Soul-Healing Plan was very profitable, but she needed additional help to heal her previous image of Alex. She still had trouble believing that Alex really wanted to be close to her. Donna was haunted by the feeling that he was only doing the exercises because a therapist told him to. She feared that the "old Alex" would eventually appear again and ruin all of the progress they had made. To heal these haunting feelings that couples have as they progress in therapy, Tom and I developed an exercise that deals specifically with this stubborn type of fear. This exercise, called the True Vision Exercise, is designed to help individuals who have a particularly bad or negative image of their partner begin to see him or her through God's eyes. This technique helps couples get a vision of who their partner can be in the Lord, and it also helps neutralize the reactivity that comes from the soul wounds of the past. The tendency for a person to put the unhealthy faces of their caretakers on their spouse can be alleviated by performing this exercise. Donna and Alex learned to get a true clear vision of each other after completing this exercise. Here is how they did this.

EXERCISE 3: TRUE VISION EXERCISE

Donna and Alex examined the list of commonalities they saw on their Soul Healogram. These included patterns, characteristics, and soul impressions. They then determined what conclusions they had drawn or what beliefs they had formulated as a result of living in their families. Both of them wrote these beliefs in a column on the left-hand side of their page, which they entitled "Beliefs." They then developed a verdict as to whether these beliefs were true or false and wrote their verdict under the middle column entitled, "Verdict."

To decide a verdict, a person must find evidence, proof, or the truth about their situation, as best they can determine it. John says, "Then you will know the truth, and the truth will set you free" (8:32). You see in Scripture that truth can provide freedom. This truth is not just the truth of the Gospel but also the truth about your perceptions of life, love, and your spouse. Determining the truth about your partner can truly set you free. Ephesians says, "Therefore each of you put off falsehood and speak truthfully to his neighbor, for we are all members of one body" (4:25). Your old brain and reactivity can create falsehoods about your spouse that can be hard to heal. They can cause you to make up realities about your partner that may not be accurate. Satan, the deceiver, can also whisper falsehoods about your spouse in your ear. The truth is what contradicts these falsehoods and creates a new and positive image of your spouse.

So how do you go about determining the truth? Here are a few ways we recommend. This part of the exercise will require that you move into the logical, rational left side of the brain. Under the column marked "Evidence," write down all the objective observable realities that you know to be true. List all the evidence you can to prove that your impression or idea is true. You may use what your partner says and does, Scripture, and prayer as means of determining the truth as objectively as possible. Let's use Donna and Alex as an example to show you how the True Vision Exercise works.

Donna's and Alex's True Vision Exercises

In her Soul Healogram, Donna saw women as responsible for keeping marriages together. Men, in turn, were distant and aloof. The conclusion she drew was that women care more than men about their marriages. She also had a soul impression that her father was unfaithful. The false beliefs she formulated from this were that men cannot be faithful, and Alex may be unfaithful to her as well. Donna listed these beliefs on the far left side of a sheet of paper under the column marked "Beliefs." She then determined whether each belief was true or false and wrote her verdict after every belief she had formulated. She also found evidence to verify her verdict. She listed these things under the column marked "Evidence" on the right-hand side of the page.

Alex learned from his Soul Healogram that he had developed false beliefs that women suffocated men and wanted to control things to get their way. He thought marriage was confining and took away a man's freedom. He listed these beliefs in a column on the left of his page and determined a verdict as to their validity. He then wrote realities or truths that validated his new beliefs about his marriage on the right-hand side of his paper. The following are examples of what Donna and Alex wrote:

Donna's True Vision Exercise

Belief	Verdict	Evidence
Men cannot be faithful.	True	In my parents' marriage.
	False	Some men find fidelity important.
Alex cannot be faithful to me.	False	Alex states that he values fidelity.
		Alex has always been faithful.
Alex is like all the men in my family and does not want to spend time with me.	False	Alex is working on goals to spend time with his family.
		Alex will go to counseling to learn how to do this.
All marriages in my family are unhappy and mine will be too.	False	Our marriage has a chance to work because we will consciously work on it.
		Alex and I demonstrate every day that our marriage is important and that working on our happiness is a priority.
		No one in my family ever did this.

Alex's True Vision Exercise

Belief	Verdict	Evidence
Women suffocate men and want control.	False	Donna says she does not want control.
Women want their way.	True	With my mother, mostly.
	False	Donna is working on her control issues in counseling.
Marriage is confining to men.	True	In my parent's marriage.
	False	In my marriage. Although Donna desires closeness, she wants to give me freedom.
Marriage takes away a man's freedom.	False	Our marriage will add to our lives, not take away from them, because we will work very hard at it in counseling.

Donna was instructed to read her evidence or truths several times daily, particularly when she feared that the "old Alex" would return. There were many more false beliefs that Donna and Alex had to correct, as they became loving and willing partners to help each other. By doing this exercise, you can see how Donna and Alex had to deal with their "old brainers," their negative soul impressions, and reactivity simultaneously. It became apparent to Donna and Alex while doing this that their issues impacted each other in an extremely destructive way. The problems Alex discovered as wounds for him were the very things that threw Donna into a tailspin and made her feel that Alex did not care about her.

It was easy for them to see why they felt so desperate and thought of divorce. Because their own wounds impacted each other in such a negative way, they thought the answer to their problem was to find a different mate. This notion is typical for couples who have not come to the awareness that any mate they select is likely to have the same wounds and impact them in the same painful way.

Individuals actually unconsciously gravitate toward people with similar wounds. This is the notion we discussed earlier called interactivity. People are actually attracted to others who have wounds that are similar to their own, but who may have opposite adaptations to those wounds. The person with a fear of abandonment is typically attracted to the person with a fear of engulfment. This is based on a theory of mating that opposites attract, or that we are attracted to those qualities that are missing or deficit within ourselves. This creates the classic pursuer/distancer marital dyad.

Take Donna and Alex for example. Donna did not consciously know that Alex had a fear of being engulfed or that he needed distance, but she did admire his independence, strength, and the fact that he could stand alone so securely. Little did she know that these qualities would be carried out in their marriage as his struggle for space and freedom from her. Eventually these independent qualities were the characteristics that hurt Donna the most. We see the same phenomenon with Donna's fear of abandonment and her clinging to Alex. At first he thought she was loving and affectionate, but soon he grew to resent her need for closeness. What they both realized through learning about interactivity was *the fact that they can wound each other so harshly means that they have more power to heal each other.*

In fact, Alex was the most powerful person to heal Donna, and Donna was the most potent healer for Alex. This intimate enemy, with whom they struggled, actually held the key to their healing. Donna and Alex worked hard to catch a true vision of each other, which set them free to see themselves and each other in a more positive light. Donna began to see Alex as wounded instead of withholding, afraid instead of aloof, and hurting instead of distant. Alex, in turn, saw Donna as scared instead of demanding, hurting instead of whiny, and wounded instead of suffocating. After several months in therapy, neither was tempted to put the wrong faces on their partners or to make up false realities about each other again. Their extreme reactivity and negative soul impressions about each other and marriage began to disappear. They directed their energy toward healing each other's souls and thus became very good friends and lovers.

If you grew up in a home that contained a great deal of dysfunction, your tendency toward false beliefs about your mate will be very high. I remember when we were dating, Tom would commit some minor offense like being late to pick me up, and I would accuse him of something outrageous like not loving me. I drew a pretty harsh conclusion from such a small crime. He, on the other hand, would have a great deal of trouble seeing me as his friend if we were in conflict. The True Vision Exercise was very helpful for us to learn to see each other in a healthier, more realistic light.

EXERCISE 4: THE RELATIONSHIP UPDATE

After couples have made great realizations about themselves and their marriage, and after they have made a Soul-Healing Plan, then they must develop a way to monitor these goals. It is paramount that couples have time alone together. We cannot tell you how many times couples come in to see us because their marriage is in trouble and we find that they have not spent quality alone time with each other in years. It seems obvious that for any relationship to grow you must at least see each other, but couples in trouble often forget this. This time alone not only helps you focus solely on each other, it is also a good time to conduct a *Relationship Update.*

We designed the Relationship Update as a time to look at your individual goals and your Soul-Healing Plan and assess how you are doing. If you are making progress, then plan a celebration. If you are lagging, use this time to determine why and what you will do about it. You may need to readjust your goals to be more realistic. You may need to add more time in order to achieve them.

Any good business has regular staff meetings, but in marriage we have a tendency to falsely assume that if we love each other, everything will just work out naturally. The Relationship Update provides a concrete way to make this happen.

One small note here: The Relationship Update is not to be used to ambush your spouse or gang up on him or her in a critical fashion. It is merely supposed to be a time to get an update on previously set goals. All too often we see spouses use alone time to have "talks," usually meaning one lectures and criticizes, and the other gets defensive and withdraws. Remember, this exercise is supposed to be a positive experience!

One very powerful experience for the soul is that of falling in love. There is no feeling like it. We become intoxicated with the presence of our beloved. We crave encounters with them. Unfortunately, many of these encounters end up in misery and pain. Setting goals as a couple and developing a Soul-Healing Plan can help couples when they go astray, but it is also good to understand more of what this in-love feeling is all about. So, we are dedicating the next chapter to the soul in love, to teach you how to help love stay the positive soul-healing experience it started out to be.

Chapter 6

The Soul in Love

In previous chapters you saw how couples slide so far down the mountain of love that they may even feel that their choice of a partner was wrong. Feelings such as "Maybe I've got the wrong man" or "Maybe this woman is not for me" can be disturbingly common for couples in marital conflict.

You saw how the principle of interactivity operates, and how one partner's woundedness impacts the other's. If they can hurt each other so badly, then why did they pick each other in the first place? What drew them to each other? What was the attraction to someone who could wound them so savagely? This chapter will try to explore and answer these disturbing questions.

George and Margaret's Story

George met Margaret at a church group. It was Margaret's first time in the group, George was sure, because he would have remembered a vision as lovely as she. His eyes met hers, and it happened, a fleeting glance, a subtle smile of approval, and then the famous double take. It was sheer destiny that they floated toward each other, totally oblivious to everyone else in the class. Their eyes fixated on each other. With hearts beating fast and palms sweating, they gaped in nervous silence. George had a large dry lump in his throat as he spoke, "You're new here, aren't you."

"Why, yes, I am," Margaret replied. After the proper but somewhat awkward introductions, they never heard another word the group leader said. They were too busy listening to each other's heart pounding.

Romantic Love

What is this wonderfully buoyant, radiant, yet anxiety-provoking feeling? What is it that causes one's heart and soul to receive a strong wallop at the sight of a prospective lover? Some call it attraction, some infatuation, some simply lust, and others romantic love.

This mystery has caused Tom and me to embark on a seemingly endless quest for what constitutes love. What is this feeling? Why do we feel it? Why do we feel it with some people and not with others? What is soul mating? Is falling in love real? Is there a difference between falling in love and choosing to love?

These are the questions that prompted our search for the holy grail of romance. We discovered several theories about love that were insightful and began to answer many of our haunting questions about relationships. By sharing these various theories with you, perhaps we can all begin to see why the heart does what it does when it is in love. A good place to start is where romantic love started. Our culture did not always embrace the notion of falling in love. For years, marriages were arranged or transacted like business deals or property settlements. So how did our society get into this agitational game of feelings and chance? Here is how the journey began.

The Origin of Romantic Love

According to Paul Gray in his 1993 *Time* magazine article, romantic love started in the twelfth century with the appearance of the troubadours and their love ballads in southern France. This was known as "courtly love," in which the theme of male supplication and entreaty of the female became popular. The troubadours would humbly petition the attention and admiration of the women in the castles, creating "courts of love." The philosophy rendered that love was attainable only outside of marriage and often only if there was no sexual communion (48).

Romantic love arose thanks to the amenities peculiar to the West. Leisure time, a modicum of creature comfort, and a certain level of refinement in the arts and literature caused romance to flourish. In places where the trappings of ease and convenience were absent, so was romance. In these westernized societies, peasants mated, and aristocrats fell in love. Thus an elaborate ritual developed between the idle noblewomen, whose husbands were away in the Crusades, and their aspiring suitors. But these swains would have been torn to bits if there had been any hint of physical consummation. The origin of romance was dictated by the needs of society and did not involve sex at all. Sociologists believe that romantic love became a part of our culture when the world evolved to a more democratic society with freedom to make more personal choices. Choosing a love partner, as opposed to being assigned one in an arranged marriage, then became fashionable (Gray 49).

So this is the origin of our current way of mating, a fantasy relationship between forbidden would-be lovers that is full of flirtation, myth, and wanting, with virtually no basis in reality and no chance of consummation, two bored people playing at a pretend relationship that has no real authenticity or actuality.

Learning the roots of romantic love was somewhat troubling for Tom and me. As therapists, we see countless individuals who live, breathe, eat, and sleep just to get a taste of this romantic bliss, and it is simply a myth and a fantasy after all. It's no wonder people in our culture say they are unfulfilled in love. What they are searching for has its roots in lunacy and aberration, not in solid reality, consciousness, or health. Sometimes we think our society would do better in those ancient arranged marriages. Perhaps the notion that one had to stay in a marriage would stop the insipid search for the perfect lover that so consumes our society since those illustrious troubadours in the twelfth century.

Romantic love is not just the plague and balm of our culture. Anthropologists have found evidence of romantic love in at least 147 other cultures (Gray 50). As you can see, Tom and I are not alone in our societal dilemma of adapting romance so it can have a healthy outcome for its constituents. Since we cannot change the modern way mates are selected in our society, or in any other culture for that matter, we are left to work with what we have. The goal, then, is to enhance romantic love and to make it healthier and more conscious for those who wish to drink from its well. We want to help those mystical would-be lovers learn all that they can about the theories of romantic love.

Theories of Romantic Love

There are almost as many theories of romantic love as there are ways of choosing a mate. These theories run the gamut from physical and sexual attraction to chemistry, biology, and projection. Even so, they help shed light on a very complex subject.

The Theory of Eros

The first theory of romantic love is based on *Eros*. Many in Western civilization think Eros is the burning ember of passion between a man and a woman. Eros is sensual and sexual in nature; therefore, a key piece of this theory of romance is physical and sexual attraction. Another name for it could even be lust. When you see someone across the room and you find yourself strongly attracted to him or her, Eros or its more lustful properties are operating. You may meet someone who looks like "your type." There are certain physical characteristics, coloring, style, movements, gestures, and posturings that create desire and make you want to get close to that person. This is Eros at work.

In his book *Finding the Love of Your Life*, Dr. Neal Warren states that many relational psychologists feel that building a deeper relationship is impossible without the physical attraction and excitement that come from passionate love. He sees this passionate love (or Eros) between two people as a critical ingredient if they are to have a long, satisfying relationship (87). While Eros is important in the mating process, many people in our society make it the litmus test for true love and negate other very significant mating factors. Thus, when attraction fades and passionate love wanes, the commitment is in danger of fading as well.

As relationship therapists, we have found Eros to be a very misunderstood concept. The Greeks knew Eros had its sensual and sexual qualities, but the true meaning of the word is only sexual in part. In the original Greek, the word *Eros* is defined as "life breath" or "life energy." This is a far cry from basic passionate love or simple fleshly lust. Yet, in our workshops when we ask participants what they think of when we use the term *Eros*, most say things like erotic, sexy, sleazy, and pornographic. The images brought to mind are seedy and perverse. The Greeks knew that people needed to feel life force or life energy, and they found it in many forms, not just sex. Literature, poetry, sports, building, talking, sharing, and just creating were ways for them to express their Eros. Westerners have reduced Eros to what most people do to play as adults—have sex. They have sexualized their life energy and think of finding their Eros in sexual fantasy, which usually suggests illicit sexual bliss. There is a subtle attitude in our culture that truly exciting fantasy-like sex cannot happen in a relationship with one's own committed lifetime partner.

Tom and I see Eros in another light. We view it more from the avenue of soul and not just the physical self. Because of this, it need not be diluted or perverted as it has been for so long in our culture. Mating and lovemaking need to be done with the soul, as well as with the body. Sexual intimacy is a sacred ritual that touches the heart of God as he blesses the lives of his children. Sex, then, is a sacred soul gift. When we view sex in this way, then Eros is desexualized and can truly represent life energy or life force in humans. The goal of marriage is to provide that life energy to yourself and your mate by learning about the soul and becoming committed to doing the things that would bring healing to it. The process of mating is a soulful process. Lovemaking is an act of soulfulness between a man and a woman, replicating our own closeness to the Lord.

Sensual Eros and physical attraction are important in the mating process. But in learning how to truly love the soul of your mate and in allowing them to love yours, they need to take a backseat to other more spiritual, soulful aspects of partnering.

The Dreamed-About Love

Early in life we formulate a vision of our "ideal mate." This vision involves physical characteristics, body shape, facial appearance, smell, skin texture, hair color, and certain personality traits. We then search for this "ideal mate," hoping to find a match. Sometimes this is done with physical appearance alone, but sometimes with a touch or a kiss. Romeo and Juliet represent this type of love-at-first-sight encounter. Dr. Neal Warren says that this "dreamed-about love" enhances our self-esteem, partially because their love makes us feel good about ourselves and partially because we feel connected to someone else (81–90).

It is because of this preexisting image of our prospective mate that we pick certain people and leave others behind. Although it is true that people have a mental grid that includes who they may be attracted to, this apparition of the "dreamed-about love" is not all there is in the mating process. This leads us to another theory of mating called the Imago.

The Theory of Imago

Dr. Harville Hendrix has done groundbreaking work in the development of Imago Relationship Theory. *Imago* is Latin, meaning "image" or "image of." Dr. Hendrix believes that we are attracted to the unconscious image of the negative and positive traits of our primary caretakers. He calls this image our Imago. The theory espouses that we are unconsciously attracted to these negative traits in order to get these prospective mates to embody the positive traits of our primary caretakers. Thus we can "create" the positive caretakers we want so desperately. This entire process is on a subconscious level, but it explains why we see so many people pick mates who replicate characteristics in their family of origin that defy logic. An example might be the daughter of an abusive alcoholic who unconsciously selects an alcoholic husband. This woman may vow that she will never marry a man like her father. She may even look for a prospective husband at Al-Anon meetings in hopes of finding a man who does not drink, but she still is at high risk for picking a partner who has some form of addiction.

One of the premises of the theory is the old Freudian notion of "repetition compulsion." This is the tendency to repeat patterns in life that are familiar to our unconscious memory. In other words, we are not fully aware of our hidden need to relive that which is familiar and comfortable. The Imago serves as an unconscious homing device that causes us to be attracted to those individuals who enable us to repeat patterns in our childhood and perhaps "get them right" this time. We are attracted to a person who can heal our childhood wounds and give us the love we have always wanted. This explains why, when we fall in love, we feel a familiarity and a comfort around our loved one that has a mystical quality. The feeling that "I have known you all my life" is part of our unconscious homing instinct that helps heal our woundedness. This soulful desire for healing is the driving force behind the relationship.

Another premise of Imago theory is that we are attracted to individuals who have complementary adaptations to the socialization process. In simpler terms, we are attracted to individuals who have similar wounds but different ways of dealing with them. We become paired with incompatible partners to create chemistry for growth. We are attracted to what is missing or lost in ourselves. The shy boy will be extremely attracted to the social butterfly. Being with her makes him feel more socially adept. Thus his woundedness can be healed in her presence. The easily embarrassed female who has trouble showing affection in public meets the handsome guy, who is free with his public displays of affection, and she feels a stimulation that she has never felt before. Hendrix says:

> Chances are that the people you are drawn to and admire possess qualities that you long for, or that were dismissed and disdained in your home. If you get close to such people, you feel good about yourself, more complete, through association. In the presence of our opposites, we can retrieve our missing parts and feel whole (*Keeping* 162).

I must admit I was skeptical of this theory at first, thinking that my husband was nothing like my extremely dysfunctional caretakers. With further exploration and some training in Dr. Hendrix's work, however, I was stunned to see there was a huge correlation between the characteristics of my family of origin and Tom. I was equally surprised when I saw that I could replicate many of the negative characteristics of my in-laws. Thank goodness I have quite a few of their positive characteristics as well.

I also noticed that Tom possessed some of the lost or missing parts of me. When I met Tom, I was nonassertive and passive. I noticed that he was able to send his undercooked steak back in a restaurant or confront a rude salesperson. When I was with him, I felt whole, complete, and more protected. He was the embodiment of my opposite. He had characteristics that I was lacking. On the other hand, I was more giving and would contribute money to various mission and charitable organizations. Tom admired this, because he had a built-in skepticism for many support-funded organizations. Being with me helped him feel more trusting and philanthropic. He felt complete in my presence, as if that part of him was redeemed.

The downside of the Imago is that while the potential partner is seen as the glorious healer of our childhood wounds, they also possess the characteristics that could deeply wound our souls. Imagine that the person who has the greatest power to bring healing to your soul also has the same power to murder your soul. Because of this, raptured lovers can end up becoming bitter enemies. In fact, we have noticed that the degree of bitterness a couple feels after a breakup is directly proportional to the degree of love or need that they once felt in the relationship. This power to wound one's partner is what constitutes marital contempt.

Tom and I have seen this resentful contempt firsthand. We both came from divorced homes. Tom's parents were married twenty-six years. Together they created two talented, bright, attractive children. They had twenty-six Christmases, twenty-six vacations, and a great many memories. At one point they were partners, lovers, and friends, yet now they are bitter enemies. The same is true for my parents. Even after four children and eleven years as a married couple, they have not spoken to each other in thirty-five years. It baffles me how they can love someone enough to marry them, have children with them, share the most intimate of life experiences with them, only to relegate them to the vitriolic position of archenemy. I am amazed at how the line between love and hate is so tentative. The same positive energy of Imago's bonding power can acidify and poison a marriage.

Dr. Hendrix's theory of the conscious relationship is designed to solve this problem. He believes that becoming aware of the woundedness in yourself and your spouse can help you become better, more conscious marriage partners. As you become aware of your mate's hurts and pains, you will be less likely to harm him or her in these areas. Preventing couples from reinjuring old childhood wounds goes a long way toward healing (228–32).

The Theory of Chemistry or Limmerence

To this point, we have evaluated our erotic mating rituals and looked at our Imago, it is now time to evaluate what part chemistry plays in a relationship.

What is chemistry anyway? We all know what we think it is. It's that giddy feeling we get when we see a certain someone. We feel weak-kneed, breathless, and oftentimes shaky. We do a double take and are compelled to get just one more glance or to ask one more inane question. The feeling that pulsates throughout our bodies is known as chemistry. The term *chemistry* has its roots in alchemy, a form of science and philosophy made popular in the Middle Ages, when alchemists were attempting to discover an elixir for life. Alchemists philosophized about the seemingly magical process that transformed ordinary materials into something of true merit. The term *chemistry* was coined to describe two common ordinary humans interacting with such energy that there was true merit in their encounter or, more accurately, true love. In her book *Love and Limmerence*, Dorothy Tennov calls this blissful state of feeling as if you can walk on air *limmerence*:

> ...the sense that one has found the key to happiness in the presence of their partner. There is an acute longing for reunification, an aching in the chest, followed by obsessive and intrusive thoughts about the loved one. There is an initial attraction and excitement that causes one to see his or her partner as utterly wonderful.

These feelings of chemistry or limmerence can also be described less mystically as a simple sympathetic understanding, harmonious interaction, or solid rapport. Limmerence helps explain statements like these: "My new love can finish my sentences," "He seems to know what I am thinking," "We are like two musical instruments playing in intimate harmony," "I feel understood by her," "I have told him things I have never shared with anyone." These are the illustrious manifestations of chemistry.

Chemistry, however, is not all it is claimed to be. It can be very unhealthy for people who only have chemistry for "losers," or for codependents who only have chemistry for people they can fix. I once had a client who realized that she only had chemistry for men who needed her. Consequently, she kept picking men who were irresponsible and dependent. When she would meet a man who was very giving and interested in her, she found him boring and would be disappointed because there was no spark.

Although some chemistry is necessary for a relationship to grow, it needs to be examined to determine whether it is healthy. If you find that you are attracted to a certain "type," and that "type" is always hurting you, you may need to alter the amount of chemistry you deem necessary to feel the relationship can grow deeper. Jan's story is a prime example.

Jan's Story

Jan came to our office because her fiancé broke off their engagement one month before the wedding. She was severely depressed and suicidal.

"I have nothing to live for," she cried, "Michael was my whole life. After three years he decided that he didn't have what it took to be married to me. I guess I was just too hard to love."

Michael was not the first man to leave Jan. She described a series of relationships in which she was strongly attracted to men who were distant, aloof, and critical. She and her girlfriends had a saying that "nice guys are a dime a dozen." In other words, if he wasn't a challenge, she did not want to pursue him.

While exploring Jan's background, it came as no surprise to us that her father was an alcoholic. She was the oldest of three children whom she cared for when her father was drunk. She described her father as handsome, energetic, and fun when he was sober. But when he drank, he withdrew and became moody, sullen, and critical. As the oldest child, Jan felt responsible to pull him out of his withdrawal. She loved to make him laugh when he was drinking, in hopes that he would interact more with the family and not be so sullen.

Jan learned early to associate chemistry and attraction with getting a seemingly distant man to pay positive attention to her. As you can see, she was playing out the same dynamics from her interaction with Dad in her adult dating relationships. She was caught in a repetition compulsion from her childhood. Thus she unconsciously selected men with whom she would have to replay the same childhood struggles. There was tremendous chemistry with these men, but they were deadly for her self-esteem, not to mention that they never truly committed to her.

In counseling Jan learned to see that she needed to consciously select men who were more loving and much less challenging. This meant she would probably have to settle for less chemistry. There would still be an attraction, I told her, but her encounters would not pack as much punch. At first this was hard for her, but what kept her trying was the lingering pain she felt after each breakup.

Eventually Jan felt comfortable with a more moderate level of chemistry; that was when she met Bobby. He was much more introverted than her previous beaus, but he was also much more emotionally and physically available. Once Jan got past the "nice guy" phenomenon, she found that Bobby was quite interesting. Her feeling that nice guys were boring, or "a dime a dozen," began to fade. It was great to see Jan start to feel at ease with being loved and cared for. She learned that she no longer had to play out the struggles of her childhood. To make a long story short, Jan and Bobby were married and committed to being soul healers for a lifetime. Jan will be the first to tell you that chemistry can be very misleading in the mating process.

One of the biggest problems with chemistry is that it fades. Just ask anyone who has been married for a while. We have even noticed this in our own marriage. The newness wears off, and some of the thrill passes. No longer do you wait for your spouse with bated breath. You don't get as tingly when he or she enters the room. Because chemistry tends to decline or weaken, many relational theorists are stressing that less emphasis should be placed on the feelings of being in love and more emphasis on the conscious decision to love one's partner. They focus on the fact that love is more of a choice than a feeling, and emotions should play a more secondary role in the mating process.

As we begin to examine what part chemistry should play in mate selection, it would be valuable to look at some recent research in the field of neurobiology that shows a biological link between our heads and our hearts, especially where chemistry and falling in love are concerned.

The Biology of Love

Have you ever wondered why you have such strong physiological triggers when you fall in love with someone? What makes your heart pound? Why do you feel butterflies in your stomach? The feeling that you can walk on air, the lack of need for food or sleep, the superhuman feeling that comes with more adrenaline—these are all physical signs of love. Why do these manifestations occur? Some people believe that they are a sure sign of true love. I once believed this myself, but recent developments in neurobiology may show us differently.

In her article "The Right Chemistry," Anastasia Toufexis states that when a person falls in love, his or her brain is flooded with chemicals. These include norepinephrine, dopamine, and especially phenylethylamine (PEA for short). All are chemical cousins to amphetamines, thus explaining the superhuman quality of falling in love. A meeting of the eyes, a touch of the hands, or a whiff of scent sets off a flood that starts in the brain and races along the nerves and throughout the bloodstream. The results are familiar: flushed skin, sweaty palms, and heavy breathing. Above all, there is the sheer euphoria of falling in love. This explains why we have such an altered physical state when we fall in love. It also helps us put the notion of falling in love in a clearer, more rational perspective.

Now that we know that PEA will blast through our systems when we are in the presence of someone who could be a potential partner, we can consciously and sanely decide if we want to pursue this relationship. We no longer have to assume that our biological triggers should dictate who our lifetime partners will be. We also do not have to overlook those potential partners who do not cause the whistle to blow as hard in the PEA factory. Humankind no longer has to be a slave to biological signals when it comes to love. This is good news for this generation of would-be partners, because further research suggests that brain-chemical highs, laced with phenylethylamine, do not last. As with any other chemical, the body begins to develop a tolerance. It then takes more and more of the substance to produce love's special kick. After two or three years, the body simply can't crank out the needed amount of PEA. This makes passionate romantic love short-lived. Fizzling chemicals spell the end of delirious passion. For many people, this marks the end of the relationship as well. This scenario is especially true for "attraction junkies," who crave the intoxication of falling in love so much that they move frantically from relationship to relationship just as soon as the first rush of infatuation fades (50–51).

In premarital counseling sessions, we ask couples to name their worst fear. So many times they say they are worried that the wonderful giddy feeling of being in love will fade. We now know that not only will it fade but it is a biological necessity. The body builds up a tolerance to PEA and simply cannot crank out enough of it to produce the sizzle it once did. Besides, the constant flow of these natural "amphetamines" places a great deal of stress on the body. When we fall in love, our neurological systems are stressed. The body cannot take this kind of stress indefinitely. This feeling needs to fade, not only to give our bodies a break but also to make room for real, sane, conscious, willful, soul-healing love.

Toufexis also adds that biology gives us a reward for long-term committed love. The brain's pituitary gland secretes endorphins, natural painkillers that give lovers a sense of security, peace, and calm. This is why we feel so horrible when a partner dies. We do not have our daily hit of "narcotics." Oxytocin is a chemical that is released many times when long-term couples make love. Many scientists call it the "cuddle chemical." It gives couples a sensation that all is right with the world (51). So, you see, if you hang on after the phenylethylamine has faded, you will get the chance to take advantage of one of nature's other more soothing remedies. Commitment does have its rewards.

The last theory of romantic love is perhaps the most complex. Although it may be difficult to grasp at first, it may offer some excellent information on love that may be helpful to you.

The Theory of Projection

The Theory of Projection has its inception in the premise that we each carry in our soul both masculine and feminine characteristics. This has important implications for the relationship between the sexes. Men typically project their feminine side onto women they are attracted to, and women typically project their masculine side onto men they are attracted to. Wherever projection occurs, the person who carries the projected image is extremely overvalued. The real person is greatly obscured by the projected image. In other words, females who have not embraced their masculine characteristics may put these onto men who are possible mates. Likewise, men who have not embraced their feminine side may project this onto women. The person who carries this projected psychic image of another has a great deal of power over that person. As long as a part of a person's psyche is perceived in someone else, that person has some form of control over the perceiver. At first the prospective partner may feel valued and flattered to be seen in such a positive light. They are willing to identify themselves with the powerful images that are projected onto them because it is an escape from the humbler task of recognizing the genuine boundaries of their real personalities.

When a woman projects her positive masculine side onto a man, she may have a delusional image of him as savior, hero, and spiritual guide, all rolled into one. She overvalues him, is fascinated by him, and is mystically drawn to him. She sees him as the ultimate man or the ideal lover. She is completed only through him; she is whole only in his presence. What is lost is now found. Through him, she has found her soul. She is content to be a loving moth around his flame. What she is not seeing, however, is that she has abandoned her search for the positive masculine qualities within herself. She has displaced them onto her ideal man and therefore does not have to find them, or refine them within herself. Her quest for the perfect love may just shortcut her own personal growth (Sanford 13).

Because this feeling of love is based purely on projections, this state of being in love is delusional; it is not based on reality. People fall in love with an image, not a real person. In his book *Invisible Partners*, Dr. John Sanford says that:

> Relationships founded exclusively on the being in-love-state can never last.... The inability of the state of being in love to endure the stress of everyday life is recognized by all great poets. This is why Romeo and Juliet had to end in death. It would have been unthinkable for Shakespeare to have con-

cluded his great love story by sending his loving couple to Sears to buy pans for the kitchen. They would have quarreled in an instant over what frying pan to choose and how much it was going to cost, and the whole beautiful story would have evaporated (15).

Summary

To summarize these theories of romantic love, we see that we can pick a partner on the basis of attraction, chemistry, limmerence, phenylethylamine (PEA), our Imago, our dreamed-about mate, or our projections. All of this has taught us that falling in love is not a rational or conscious process. It is not based on reality. You saw that falling in love and out of love is even more "insane" than we think. Therefore, we are left with one conclusion: True soul-healing love is a sane, rational, conscious process of choice. It involves an act of the will, not just of the heart. Soul-healing love is a commitment of soul that is rooted in decision more than in flighty feelings. It is indeed hard work, but it is worth it. The next chapter is committed to showing you how to do this difficult, yet fulfilling, work.

Chapter 7

Making Love Work

Mary and Lou had been married for fourteen years. They had the American dream: two kids, two cars, a big house complete with a big mortgage, and a successful business that kept them both very busy. Mary called our office because she wanted Christian marriage counseling. It seemed that several years before their good friends, Ricky and Lucy, were on the verge of divorce and came to see us. They had attended a Soul Healers Workshop and began to mend their marriage.

Mary felt their marriage needed a face-lift, and Lou reluctantly agreed. In the first session it was obvious that Mary was the expressive, emotional part of this duo. She did most of the talking and Lou would nod and respond in a logical, matter-of-fact manner. Both described their marriage as sagging. They shared that they were distant from each other and that their communication was stilted. Their family history revealed that Mary was the eldest of two children. Her younger brother, Murray, was a very rebellious teenager who had become a drug addict during his adolescence. He was what we call in family therapy the "identified patient." She stated that Murray was still causing the family grief by continuing to live in a very unhealthy manner. He typically drifted from job to job and still had a drug habit. Mary had always played the role of caretaker for her younger brother, which established codependent patterns very early in her life. Mary also played the role of "family hero," in which she was responsible for upholding the good name of the family. While Murray was tearing the family down by playing the bad kid, Mary was responsible for building it up by playing the good kid. She made straight As, was the drum majorette of the band, president of the honor society, and was an all-around exemplary child. Her mother's favorite statement to her was, "You have never given me a minute's worth of trouble," and the implied message was, "You must be good at all costs." Performing for love and acceptance became a way of life for Mary.

Lou was the youngest of four boys. He grew up in Philadelphia in a rough neighborhood and got into trouble early in life. He quit school when he was sixteen and ran the streets. He drank and used drugs regularly. After a brush with the law, his father convinced him to join the army to get some "discipline." In the military, he finished high school and got a college education. When he left the army, he landed a great job in a high-pressure sales firm. Because he was a natural salesman, he went straight to the top. He was making great money and things were finally going his way.

Then he met Mary. It was love at first sight. They couldn't get enough of each other. He wined and dined her at the finest restaurants. They traveled to exotic places. He even took her to Vail, Colorado, for two weeks and patiently taught her to ski. They had a whirlwind romance. On the chemistry scale of one to ten, they said they were an eleven. We shared with them that brain chemicals such as phenylethylamine were released when a person falls in love, and both agreed that their PEA levels were significantly high.

Mary remembered seeing some hints of Lou's irresponsibility while they dated. There were times when he hadn't gone into the office and failed to return phone calls from clients, but she chalked this up to his being in love and wanting to spend all the time with her that he could. Lou would get back on track and settle down after they were married. Mary was sure of it. In six months they were married. Mary had plans of settling down and establishing more of a routine. Lou still wanted to travel and play.

"We can't afford to keep up this lifestyle," she would plead. "We need to save money for our future."

"Let's live for the moment. We have plenty of time to settle down. Don't be such a party pooper," Lou would reply.

And so the honeymoon was over and the power struggle started, with Mary wanting to establish a more conservative lifestyle, and Lou wanting to live unencumbered. Gradually they began to drift apart.

After about two years, Mary felt the magic and chemistry start to fade. She feared that maybe she had made a mistake. Maybe she had married the wrong man. She kept this fear deep inside and, being the over-responsible person she was, decided to do everything she could to make her marriage work. Very soon she got pregnant and William was born. She now had something to consume her time and interest. She loved being a mother, and Will's birth seemed to bring her and Lou closer. Mary poured herself into parenting. Will became her main focus. She did not want him to turn out like her brother, and she was determined not to make her parents' mistakes. Lou began to feel more and more neglected. He started hanging out after work with some fellow sales reps. They frequented a local pub regularly. Before he knew it, Lou was drinking every night and excessively on the weekends. When Mary confronted Lou, he got defensive or denied that he had a problem. He told her that if she would pay more attention to him when he was home, maybe he wouldn't stay out with his friends.

Finally, Lou stopped coming home at all on Friday nights. This went on for several months, and one Saturday Mary got a concerned phone call from Lou's boss. He told Mary that Lou's work was slipping, and his attendance was poor. He suspected that Lou had a drug problem. When Lou finally came home that weekend, Mary confronted him. After a huge argument, he reluctantly admitted that he had been using cocaine, and it was becoming a real problem for him.

In shock, Mary threatened to leave if he did not get help. So Lou checked himself into a local Christian treatment center. He had an experience with God and started to sober up. Things began to improve in their lives and in their marriage. They joined a local church and became very active there. It was about this time that Lou started his own business. Mary soon got pregnant with their second child, a girl. They had their family, their faith, and their health. What more could they ask for? But deep inside of Mary there was still a nagging feeling that something was missing in her marriage. When their minister preached about spiritual oneness in a marital relationship, she came home longing and depressed.

Lou's business consumed a great deal of his time, and he pressured Mary to work for him. This had been a pattern in their relationship in the past. They had had many arguments about it, which precipitated her call for counseling. It seemed that after her daughter's birth, she no longer had the drive or the stamina to work in Lou's business. It reminded her too much of the days when she was his caretaker. She wanted to devote all of her attention to being a full-time mother. Lou resented this because he felt unsupported and abandoned. He was frustrated because he said that Mary nagged him to come home all the time. If she helped him in the business, he could come home more. Mary was upset because she did not want the pressure of taking care of him any longer. She wanted him to stand on his own two feet. The more she nagged, the more distant he became. Thus we see the typical pattern of the pursuer and distancer played out in their relationship. Like many of the other couples in therapy, they were playing "marital Pac-Man."

Tom and I told Mary and Lou that marriages go through stages similar to the way children go through stages in their development. Sharing these stages with couples seems to validate and normalize their frustrated feelings about marriage and establishes a foundation for healing.

The Stages of Marriage

So many couples do not know what to expect in matrimony. Since they have no idea of what is coming next, they feel a sense of panic or even doom when the relationship shifts or changes, just as Lou and Mary did. We shared with them that every human experience has three basic phases, and marriage is no different. The beginning phase of any experience is the *expansion stage*. During this time, you are likely to feel hopeful and filled with positive expectations.

What usually comes after any new experience? *Disillusionment.* Yes, disappointment comes because some things do not work out the way you thought. The new job was not the answer to your problems. The college education did not yield the perfect career. Marriage has its own set of disappointments, yet society puts so much pressure on couples to feel positive all of the time. Any hint of disillusionment in matrimony causes you to feel that the magic has faded or that you have made the wrong choice. As marriage counselors, we counsel our clients to *expect* disappointment in marriage. Anticipate it, and then when it happens, you will not be so shocked, and you will also be strong enough to handle it.

The last stage of all human experience is *resolution*. This comes only through accepting your current state of disillusionment, and doing what you can to make a difference.

The problem with marriage is that many times couples become so disheartened that they cannot move toward healing and resolution. We have seen that making couples aware of the stages of marriage helps them normalize their fear and panic about their struggles and reach resolution about their marital frustrations and disappointments. The stages of marriage are as follows: Romantic Love, Power Struggle, Awakening, Transformation, and Reality Love.

The Romantic Love Stage

The first stage of a love relationship is *romantic love*. As you saw in the previous chapter, this stage is characterized by positive brain chemicals (PEA) and delusion. During this delusional stage, we believe our partner to be our hero, or the answer to all our problems. At this time our "chosen one" can do no wrong. I once had a client tell me that when her new boyfriend cleared up his bankruptcy, ended his probation for beating his ex-wife, and got his children back from social services, everything was going to be wonderful in their lives. Was she delusional or what? One of our workshop attendees put it best when she said, "When I first met my husband, I thought he was perfect, but now I know that my brain was just on drugs."

You learned earlier that the romantic love stage is not based on reality. It is highly emotional and full of positive projections. You want to see your partner all the time. You just can't seem to get enough of him or her. This is partially because the brain chemical, phenylethylamine, is activated in the presence of your partner and partly because you feel so secure when you are with him or her. Couples spend the whole day with each other, and go home and immediately call each other. They use pet names and talk "baby talk" to each other. Their interaction looks much like a mother or father bonding with a newborn infant. Couples use this time to bond and form an attachment as well. As couples settle into reality, their interactions become more and more routine. Warts and scars on their precious partners, that were previously undetected, now loom ominously on the horizon. These disheartened couples find that they are entering into what Harville Hendrix calls the *power struggle* stage.

The Power Struggle

This is the stage when our true love begins to let us down. We are counting on him to be our "knight in shining armor" or on her to be the "devoted moth around our flame" who will save us from all of life's ills. It is obvious why we become furious when he or she turns out to be a mere mortal. Unfortunately, the power struggle is just as delusional as the romantic love stage, but now instead of projecting all the positive characteristics onto our mate, we give him or her all the negative ones. We are sure that our mate knows what to do to love us and meet our needs, since he or she so readily and willingly did this in the romantic stage. Now we feel that our partner just stubbornly refuses to meet them. There is no fury too great for this crime. We once thought the world of our partner, but now we are arguing over toothpaste, budgets, and how many times we have made love in the last month.

Because our true love has now betrayed us, we have rancor and malice for this "villain." The sad truth is that this person is no more a "villain" than he or she is a "knight in shining armor." We are both merely human, and now we are faced with the responsibility of seeing each other as we really are. It is hard for our soul to make sense out of the sudden change in our partner, so we make up our own realities. We assign evil or negative motives to them in order to explain their unexplainable behaviors and actions toward us. We falsely accuse our mates of intentions they do not possess and of crimes they may not have committed. By doing this, we overreact, or become reactive, to the offenses committed against us.

Our couple, Mary and Lou, found their reactivity to be very high during this stage. Mary decided that Lou was just like her drug-addicted brother and was going to be irresponsible. Anytime Lou did anything that was the slightest bit irresponsible, she panicked and accused him of sabotaging his success. Lou was also reactive and decided that Mary was a "control freak" who liked to complain because it gave her a sense of power, just like his mother. Mary would nag, blame, and coerce him into hearing her point. This hit Lou's childhood wound of being a bad boy. Mary's behavior reminded him of his mother, and how she would scream at him and plead with him to stay out of trouble. Lou felt he could not do anything good enough for Mary, just as he felt with his mother when he was growing up. He was often passive-aggressive with Mary, promising her he would do something and then "forgetting" to do it. This would hit her wound of not feeling valued unless she was performing or caretaking, and she would retaliate in anger.

Once again, as in previous case examples, we see interactivity rear its ugly head. Mary's and Lou's wounds were interactive. They were constantly making impact statements that drove the knife even farther into each other's wounds. Remember, impact statements are statements made by couples out of their own woundedness which directly affect the woundedness of their spouse. These impact statements activated Mary's and Lou's old brain feelings of rejection and pain and caused even more hurt and destruction in their relationship.

It was obvious that Mary and Lou were not friends. They no longer saw each other as allies. In the power struggle stage, they became adversarial. Eros had turned sour, and even friendship, or *philia*, was not an option. Unfortunately, the power struggle stage is where most couples stay. Mary and Lou had been in it for fourteen years. They argued, fought, manipulated, and made deals. The agenda for each was to have his or her own way. The "I-will-die-for-you" courtship had turned into an "me-first" war zone.

There is a way out of the power struggle, however. It is committing to become soul healers. Becoming a soul healer takes hard work. With effort and determination, a couple can move to the next stage of marriage, or *awakening*.

The Awakening Stage

During the stage of awakening, we come to know each other for who we really are. We move from placing blame to seeing what part we play in our marital problems. We stop pointing fingers and start owning our woundedness. We ask ourselves a very important question: What is it like living with me? The focus then is turned away from our mate's warts and flaws to our own. This is not a martyrish attempt at self-blame or false humility but rather an honest and courageous attempt, with the Lord's help, to see the character flaws and negative behaviors we play out in our marriage.

During our awakening, we gather information about ourselves and our mates. This is when the Soul Healogram (see Chapter 4) can be very helpful. It provides couples with a wealth of knowledge that can prove to be beneficial in soul healing.

Mary and Lou completed the Soul Healogram and discovered several things that they had not known before. They made some excellent realizations about each other, but they still needed to pray for God's grace to see each other in a more positive light. Even after completing the True Vision Exercise (see Chapter 5), this couple still harbored ill feelings, hurt, and pain.

Hearing about each other's woundedness was new to them and made them feel anxious and disoriented. This is common for couples because they are giving up their old ways of behaving. They are now forced away from the "blame game" and dancing to the "you-don't-love-me" shuffle and are propelled toward change. This change can be very scary for couples. We tell them that it gets worse before it gets better, because these new insights and behaviors are uncomfortable for them. This discomfort causes anxiety and even fear.

After Mary and Lou completed their Soul Healogram, they were ready to formulate their Soul-Healing Plan. They were to write the goals for this plan independently of each other and then share them in therapy. Their goals are listed here:

Mary's Soul-Healing Plan Date: 2-14-96

1. That Lou and I would become soul mates and share our deep feelings with each other.

2. That Lou would take the financial responsibility for the family.

3. That I devote full-time to caring for the children and not feel guilty about not working in the business.

4. That Lou would come home from work at a reasonable hour, and spend at least one night a week having family time with the kids.

5. That we would learn to communicate better and learn to resolve conflict in a healthy manner.

Lou's Soul-Healing Plan Date: 2-14-96

1. That Mary stop nagging me about every little thing that I do.

2. That Mary stop being so angry.

3. That we have biweekly date nights and start being more playful with each other again.

4. That we have a more fulfilling sexual relationship.

5. That Mary compliment and affirm me more.

As you can see, their goals were very different. Most of Lou's goals were about Mary changing, and most of Mary's goals were lofty and somewhat philosophical. Now before you think their marriage was a lost cause, let us assure you that it is not uncommon for couples to present very different agendas in counseling. After many years as marriage counselors, we have grown to realize that what each person wants in marriage is not as important as *why* they want it.

Mary started sharing her "whys" first. She did not want to work in their family business because she was tired of feeling responsible for taking care of Lou. Mary was having trouble forgiving Lou for the past, and she felt she could not trust him be a responsible provider all on his own. She wanted to spend her time and energy taking care of her children and herself. She expressed guilt feelings for not being there for her children earlier in the marriage when she was working in the business.

Mary began to cry. Her voice softened as she poured out stories about her life growing up in a home where she felt responsible for making her parents happy. She had one of many regressive reflections during her therapy. She started feeling the pain of her childhood as if she were back there actually experiencing it. Lou got to see firsthand how painful it was for her. He began to feel her pain with her. She shared stories of her brother's addiction, how she took care of him, and often protected her parents from the truth about his problems. It did not take long for Lou to see why it was so important for Mary not to feel overburdened with financial responsibility and the pressure to fix everything.

Lou also relived painful childhood memories and had a few regressive reflections of his own. Mary sat by his side and supported him. She developed a better understanding of the little boy who never felt good enough and acted out to get attention from his parents.

Even though they were "revisioning" each other, there was still a great deal of resistance to change. Each appeared to be waiting for the other to act. No one wanted to be the first to take the risk. This is where the concept of intentionality comes in.

Intentionality is a concept used a great deal in self-help groups involving addiction. "Fake it till you make it" is the more colloquial term. In other words, *act* a certain way regardless of what you are *feeling*. Alcoholics Anonymous teaches that even if you do not feel like walking past the bar door, even when you are dying for a drink, resist it anyway. After a while, your feelings will follow your behavior. Many A.A. participants refer to this as "white knuckle sobriety"; that is, staying sober by an act of will, not emotion. We feel that many couples could use "white knuckle matrimony." In marriage, intentionality is consciously trying to change a negative behavior whether or not you have loving feelings for your mate. When couples change their behavior, positive emotions can follow. As couples learn to incorporate intentionality in their relationship they are ready to move to the next stage of marriage, called *transformation*.

The Transformation Stage

When couples reach transformation, their souls begin to shift. They no longer act on feelings and emotions but choose to use certain skills and tools to aid in better marital interaction. They learn to deal with their reactivity and negative soul impressions and to form new ideas about their spouse. No longer are couples tempted to make up realities about their partner. If they slip back into this old behavior, they know the quick road out. Couples lose that selfish edge they once had, and emotional or physical escape is no longer a pondered or real option. They close escape hatches and stop pursuing other forms of distraction from their marriage. When couples reach this stage, they begin to replicate the 1 Corinthians 13 passage about love: They are patient and kind and do not boast. They want the best for their spouse. Soul-healing love becomes a possible, visible goal on the marital horizon.

As they entered the transformation stage, Mary and Lou had to work very hard to *agape*, or unconditionally love, each other. Agape is love given to a person without he or she deserving it. It is given simply because the giver chooses to do so. God gives his children unconditional love. His gift cannot be earned and is not deserved, yet he still chooses to give it.

Mary had a hard time feeling she could give Lou unconditional love. The things he had done in the past haunted her soul and inhibited her ability to trust. This wounded Lou because he felt that Mary would hold his past sins against him forever. When she tried to talk about his drunken binges and spending sprees, he quoted Scriptures about forgiveness. He told her repeatedly that God could not forgive her if she would not forgive him. This form of "spiritual extortion" caused Mary to resent Lou and withhold love and grace from him even more. Acting intentionally with unconditional love was one of the hardest pieces of work this couple did. This kind of love involved stretching beyond their own selfishness. It also involved giving presents that were emotional and behavioral, as well as literal gifts to each other. This kind of caring between couples needs to be supported by the supernatural power of prayer.

We agreed to pray with and for this couple and ask that the Lord help them to act lovingly, to be open to God's leading, *even if they didn't feel like it*. They both "faked it till they made it," and with the Lord's help, they began to see each other through different eyes. Their behavior not only began to change, but their hearts changed as well. They had both a first- and second-order change.

In family therapy we look for two specific measures of change: behavioral and attitudinal. *Behavioral, or first-order, change* actually involves changing or reconstructing your behavior to reach a desired goal. This kind of change answers the question, Are you acting differently?

Second-order change, however, is a *change of attitude*. The operative question here is, Do you feel differently? This implies a change of the heart. Your behavior is different because you want it to be, because your heart dictates that it change. This behavior change is an outgrowth of a change in your emotions and beliefs. We call this a soul shift, or soul change.

Mary was trying very hard to make a first-order change. She was "faking it" and "making it" as hard as she could. She was sharing childhood pain, acting in a loving manner to Lou, checking her reactivity and "old brainers," and trying to be as intentional as possible. Mary had a problem, however; faking her feelings was very difficult for her. She had trouble feeling like a phony. Authenticity and truth were very important concepts in her life. I had to assure her many times that the goal of this process was not dishonesty or loss of integrity due to phoniness. The goal was simply to act lovingly and Christlike and to pray for the feelings to follow. Mary reluctantly agreed to try these new behaviors on faith.

With God's help, Mary was able to spot most of her reactivity and eventually stop it. She was able to trust the Lord and give Lou agape. By acting in obedience and love, her heart did indeed begin to change. One of the first feelings that came back was her genuine gratitude and appreciation for Lou. Compliments and encouragement began to flow naturally from her. This started to heal Lou's wound of never feeling good enough, so his soul began to shift as well. Both of them started acting and feeling more loving toward each other.

It took a while for Mary to fight through her resistance to acting phony, but it paid off in the healing of both her and Lou's souls. Their relationship then moved to the final stage of marriage, the best one, the one Harville Hendrix calls *reality love* (*Getting* 112ff).

The Reality Love Stage

This is the stage that makes all the struggles worthwhile. This is when couples have knowledge, acceptance, appreciation, and gratitude for each other. Instead of seeing their mate as a demon of destruction, they get in touch with what bonded them in the first place. We call this the stage of soul-healing love.

By giving each other God's unconditional love, couples create a safe environment for mutual sharing. Both feel freer to share their soul pain. This sharing helps them develop a deeper understanding of themselves and their spouse. Couples start "revisioning" each other as soul healers, not soul wounders. They develop compassion and empathy for the wounds in each other's souls and commit to healing them. No longer do they see the face of their perpetrators on their partner; instead, they see an innocent wounded child, and they want to nurture and heal that child.

Seeing the Wounded Child's Face

During the reality or soul-healing love stage, couples start by seeing each other as wounded children instead of difficult, frustrating adults. This "revisioning" each other is extremely helpful for couples in trouble, like Mary and Lou. Remember when they first came in to see us? They were full of anger and fear. Like most desperate couples, both felt that the other had evil or less-than-honorable intentions. They tended to reduce the problems in their marriage to selfishness on their mate's part. Blaming each other became a way of life for them. This only reinforced their negative image of each other and blinded them to the part they played in the marital conflict.

As Mary and Lou started to see the wounded child's face on each other, they stopped seeing their mate's motives so negatively and began to understand the reasons for each others' actions. They could also own responsibility for how they affected their relationship. *Koinonia*, or mutual empathy, began to emerge. They started to feel each other's pain as if it were their own. A shared respect grew between them that was rooted in a deep understanding of what each had gone through in life.

Lou listened with compassion and empathy while Mary poured out childhood wounds of a little blonde girl who had to grow up too fast. It was much more difficult for him to withdraw, get angry, or become passive-aggressive at an innocent wounded little girl who just wanted everyone to be happy. Likewise, it was hard for Mary to put an uncaring, unloving face on a little boy who got into trouble while simply looking for attention and love from his family.

So the hurting little girl who tried to over-caretake everyone and the wounded little boy who never felt good enough finally started seeing each other as friends. Caring for each other's soul was no longer a chore, or an act of the will. It became their utmost desire. Both wanted to listen as their partner shared. Both felt it was important to minister soul-healing love to each other. They became friends.

It is important to note here that *philia* or friendship is a logical progression for a couple after Eros, erotic love, and agape, unconditional love. We interviewed many Christian couples who had been married over forty years and asked them to name the most important ingredient in marriage. To our surprise, they did not say it was any great sacrificial giving or moving revelation. It was simply being friends. Many of them spoke of caring, concern, and support, but the answers boiled down to pure and simple friendship, or *philia*. We see so many couples who marry, bear children, buy homes, and share the daily grind with each other, but they are not friends. It is no wonder so many marriages are suffering today.

Mary and Lou's friendship began to bloom when they started seeing each other through different eyes. Learning about brain chemicals like PEA and the stages of marriage helped them see why their passion had fizzled. After their many insights, they were ready to learn to communicate the really negative emotions they were feeling. They were also ready to see what they did to hurt each other, learn to share this information in a healthy way, and then ask for and grant forgiveness. The next chapter shows you step by step how to do this.

Chapter 8

What's Eating You and Why

We have already learned that the state of being in love is more of a myth than a reality. It is based on projection not truth. Remember, *projection* is defined as "the act of visualizing an idea in our minds as an objective reality."[1] We learned previously that we tend to make up realities about our partner. In relationships we see things through our own clouded perspective, which may not be completely accurate. Projection can also be a way in which we cloud our perspective and attribute to another person or object feelings, thoughts, or attitudes that are present in ourselves. In the romantic stage of marriage, we have a tendency to project positive characteristics onto our partner. In the power struggle stage, we tend to project negative characteristics. By doing this, we do not have to own or deal with these characteristics within ourselves. When a problem arises in marriage, our tendency is to look outside of our own psyches and project blame onto our spouses. This may blind us to what is really eating us in our marriage and why.

Fred and Ether's Story of Projection

Fred was a thirty-year-old bachelor. He came into our counseling office because his girlfriend of two years had just broken up with him. He was not eating or sleeping, and he was so depressed that he had trouble getting out of bed in the morning.

"I feel completely lost and empty without Ethel. What am I going to do? She was my whole life. She inspired me. Now I can't even go to work."

Upon further questioning, I found that Fred saw Ethel as the life force or life energy in their relationship. Fred was raised in a stoic, conservative, sexually shaming home, so he was very shy and inhibited. Ethel was sensual and expressive. He was stiff and unaffectionate; she was warm and openly affectionate. He was too serious; she could laugh and play. No wonder Fred felt more complete and whole with Ethel, she possessed everything he had repressed. When she walked out of his life, all of his Eros, or life energy, went with her. Fred felt dead inside. To heal himself, he had to learn that he too possessed the characteristics that Ethel brought into the relationship. They were just lost to his conscious mind or repressed. It was easier and safer for Fred to project these characteristics onto Ethel than to develop them within himself.

As we learned in the previous chapter, couples often do this early in their relationship. Later, however, they tend to project negative characteristics from their psyche onto their partner. As Fred began to look inside himself, find these lost parts, and act on them, he began to feel more complete. This helped him get over Ethel and learn to love again.

Projection and Relationships

Since relationship theorists say that 80 percent of all communication is projection, it would behoove us to examine our communication in order to separate fantasy from reality, or truth from projection. These same relationship theorists say that what we despise most in others is really a projection. The qualities that we hate the most in others are those negative qualities that we possess within ourselves.

Is there a characteristic that you really scorn in others? Say that you despise arrogant people. Could it be that you have a small piece of this arrogance within yourself? Seeing your own despised psyche personified in another creates discomfort and anxiety. You feel uneasy or troubled. These are unpleasant emotions, so you have disdain for the bearer of the traits that bring out such angst in you. It is much easier for you to greatly despise in others that which you may see in small portion within yourself, because if you see it within yourself, you may have to own it and then do something about it. Rather than working toward healing within yourself, it is easier to put this off onto someone else—and who better than your spouse. After all, he or she already contains some of the positive projections of your repressed psyche. That is why couples fall in love with each other in the first place. It becomes almost second nature to "give" or project these unpleasant or negative characteristics onto your partner as well.

Communication and Projection

Since you now know that projection is a large part of communication in a relationship, it is safe to assume that the main things you dislike about your partner are also present within you. You also repress those traits that were not sanctioned in your home. Remember that Fred repressed his outgoing nature when he was younger, because his family did not approve of, or encourage, his social side. They praised his serious, academic, quiet qualities. In fact, it may not have been safe for him to be social or outgoing when he was growing up.

In the beginning of his relationship with Ethel, Fred felt safe and complete, as he was allowed to explore these repressed parts of himself in the presence of one who was gifted in the social arena. As the relationship progressed, however, her display of social prowess only pointed out his deficiency. It also made him feel unconsciously uncomfortable and even anxious, as she so openly displayed that which was not valued or supported in his home. As a result, he began to project his own lack of social graces onto her. He started accusing her of having poor social skills. This is ironic because her outgoing nature was what initially attracted him to her.

"Why do you talk so much at parties?" he would ask accusingly. "People think it's rude when they can't get a word in edge wise. No one likes a blabbermouth."

"Blabbermouth!" Ethel would retort. "Look at you. If I didn't talk, the group would die of boredom. You just sit there and never interact in the conversation."

The very things that attracted Fred and Ethel to each other, the very things that complemented their sense of wholeness, became the issues that caused conflict. The things that completed them repelled them.

As our theory of projection unfolds, we see that Fred had a repressed socialite within him and Ethel had a shy girl inside her. Seeing their partner act differently from themselves caused them to have anxiety. Rather than express this as an internal struggle, most couples share this as criticism, just as Fred and Ethel did.

To handle this type of conflict more constructively, each person needs to own their own part in their projections. This is called "leaning into your projection." If Fred could cultivate his own social nature, and Ethel could own and accept her inhibited side, then these two would bring more compassion and understanding to the table of relational discord. They would each be less apt to criticize the other and more predisposed to share genuine feelings in conflict. They would also learn the cardinal rule of relationships: *You are not your partner, and your partner is not you.* Take a moment and think about what you dislike most in your mate. Do you possess this characteristic in some measure in yourself? Can you own this? Does this give you more understanding about why your mate does what he or she does? As partners begin to apply this principle, they can learn to heal the strife and discord in their marriages.

Learning to Repress

How did we lose this natural part of ourselves in the first place? We were born with certain innate characteristics. As babies, we were loving, lovable, and playful. We had no reservations about crying at 2 A.M. when we were hungry. We were naturally expressive. When we needed something, we screamed for it. As adults, however, we have learned that certain traits were promoted, while others were discouraged. These characteristics were not necessarily what might be best for our particular *bend*, or nature. Take Fred, for example. His parents could really have helped him by encouraging his social skills and developing his extroverted side. But instead, they touted his more serious strengths, because they too were serious.

Proverbs says, "Train up a child in the way he should go. Even when he is old he will not depart from it" (22:6). The Hebrew word for way is *derek*, meaning "nature, course of life, mode of action, custom, manner or bend."[2] The Scripture is saying that we should train up children according to *their* mode or *their* bend. Train them based on their predisposed manner. Train them according to the characteristics that best support who *they* are. Many Christian parents misinterpret this passage to read "train up a child in the way I, as his parent, think the child should go." This is not accurate scripturally, nor is it good or healthy for them emotionally and psychologically.

What if your entire family were accountants, and you were expected to follow in their footsteps, yet you are greatly talented at art and hate math? What if you come from a family of athletes, and you are a weak slight-of-build child? What if you are an overachieving perfectionist and your parents insisted on pushing you too much to succeed? They could actually foster an obsessive-compulsive neurosis within you.

This is what has happened to many individuals today. Their *way* was not found, and their *bend* was not supported. Because of this, they became only shadows of their true selves. They were split off from many of their worthy attributes. This splitting off is the seedbed of much of their relational conflict as adults.

Parents are responsible for finding their child's *way* and helping the child follow it. Rather than force a child's round psyche into life's square hole, parents need to ask God, the Creator of these children, to guide them. If parents try too hard to put their own, or society's, unhealthy agenda on their children, they can cause their children to repress their most godly qualities. Here are some examples of attitudes and statements that you may have heard as a child that would cause you to repress or hide your true self.

- *Children should be seen and not heard* — causes us to repress our ability to articulate our thoughts, feelings, and actions.
- *Children should be quiet and not make noise* — causes us to split off from our ability to articulate and verbalize.
- *Children should not act silly* — causes us to repress our natural joyfulness and playful side. We become very serious.
- *If you can't say anything nice, don't say anything at all* — causes us to split from the truth within us.
- *Don't be sexual. Don't be sensual. Sex is dirty* — causes us to repress the normal, sensual side of our humanness.

Some messages are indigenous to gender.

- *Nice girls don't flirt* — causes women to repress their natural mating energy and nature.
- *Loudness or yelling or anger isn't ladylike* — causes women to repress their assertiveness.

- *Girls don't play sports. Boys are the athletes* — causes women to split off from their athletic ability.
- *Nice girls don't get angry* — causes women to split off from expression of their hurt and pain.
- *Big boys don't cry* — causes men to repress their sensitivity and compassion.
- *Boys are supposed to be tough* — causes men to repress their pain.
- *Boys should not have needs* — causes men to ignore their own soul needs and never show vulnerability.
- *Nice guys finish last* — causes men to repress their kind side and show more of their competitiveness.

Families are not the only source of soul repression. Culture and society have also played a big part in dictating some of these damaging gender rules. My grandmother is 102 years old. She grew up in the hills of Tennessee, believing that a woman's place was "barefoot, pregnant, and chained to the stove." My mother grew up in the 1930s when men were believed to have the brains, and women were the domestic ones, or caretakers. The idea of women going to college was unheard of in her small southern hometown. A college education was for men, not women. Why would a women get an education if she was going to marry? This caused the women in my family to repress their abilities, drive, and ambition, and sometimes even ignore the call of God in their lives.

Our generation is coming to terms with the war between the genders. Our children have a better chance of not repressing parts of their natural *bend*, because of society's less slanted structure. Today men take time off work to drive the kids to the pediatrician who is a woman. The change in cultural stereotypes can bring a great deal of healing to our lost selves.

Finding Our Lost Selves

We need to acknowledge what parts of us are wounded and lost, and how this happened. We can work on healing those wounds by allowing the repressed aspects of our souls to surface. Then we can bring them under the control of the Holy Spirit and allow God's mighty power to help channel these feelings, emotions, and attributes in a healthy direction.

If we stay fearful of these lost parts, the dark forbidden shadow of our souls will rear its ugly head in our marriage. In courtship the appearance of our disallowed self, which was contained within our partner, made us feel complete, but eventually that which is forbidden starts to scare us. When this happens, we attack our partner and project all the forbidden parts of our soul onto him or her. By doing this, we never have to face our own repressed aspects and learn to heal them. Projecting is about making our problem belong to our spouse. We project our psychic mess onto our spouse, so we do not have to take responsibility for facing our own discomfort and fear.

An example of this type of projection was played out early in our own marriage. Tom was working as a pastor, and I was working part-time, in private practice, as a therapist. Our first child, Mandy, was fifteen months old. It was the end of a busy day. I had picked her up from the babysitter and was preparing supper. It began to get late, and Tom was not home. Six o'clock rolled around. I called the church, but the phones had already been switched to the answering machine. It was now 6:30, and no Tom. Dinner was getting soggy, and Mandy was starting to whine. In an effort to pacify her, I gave her some Cheerios, which she promptly began to throw on the floor. The dog came in and ate all the Cheerios on the floor and on her high-chair tray. She started to scream, the oven buzzer went off, and the phone rang. It was a phone solicitor wanting me to be charitable. Needless to say, I was not feeling charitable at that time. I lost it! I fussed at the caller, then fussed at the dog, and then fussed at my precious hungry child. As you can imagine, I was feeling like a failure as a mother, a cook, and a Christian. The internal angst of my guilt was eating me alive. About 7:10 my husband arrived to our chaotic home. I launched into him with a vengeance.

"Where have you been?" I whined. "Why didn't you call to say you were going to be late?" Before he could catch his breath, I was busy projecting all my guilty feelings onto him. "What kind of husband would leave his family stranded at supper time? What kind of Daddy would leave his poor baby hungry without so much as a phone call?"

In two minutes I had successfully "given" Tom all of my guilt and agony about being a bad person. I no longer had to deal with these awful feelings, because my displaced anger at Tom allowed me to project all of them onto him. You can just imagine how he felt being welcomed into his home with this! It goes without saying that we did not have a good time in the Rodgers household that evening. We have traveled the hard road that couples take as they learn to "lean into their projections," rather than than spew them onto each other. It has taken many years on our part to really look inside ourselves and see the ugliness that we would rather "give away" to each other. We began to look at what was eating us in our relationship and why. For many couples, this can be a difficult task.

Fear and Repression

Oftentimes the people who have the hardest time owning their forbidden repressed parts are those who have what we call the "perfect Christian profile." I once possessed this nasty syndrome, so I know firsthand what it is like to feel as if you have to be a perfect Christian to receive God's blessing. Because of this, I often refused to own any of my sin nature. The guilt was much too hard to bear. The answer to all my life's struggles was to be better, work harder, or serve more. There was no room for God's grace to abound, because I was using my perfectionism and determination instead. My guilt and shame would not allow me to own the dark parts of my soul, so I had to have somewhere to put them—ah yes, how about my mate, the perfect hiding place. I'll just give him all my ugliness in the form of a projection.

Projection works just like a movie projector that puts forth an image on the screen. We put our forbidden self on the movie screen of our mate's psyche, and thus we see our lost parts portrayed or enacted by someone else. This gets us off the hook from owning and healing our own dark shadow. It also allows us to continue hiding or repressing that prohibited part of ourselves. It is then safe to say that we project onto our partner that which we fear seeing in ourselves.

EXERCISE 5: THE GIFT EXERCISE

The main way we project our own mess onto our partner is through anger. Anger is usually our mate's retaliatory response as well. We either become furious with our spouse for possessing the same behaviors that we despise in ourselves or furious with ourselves for our own dark spots. Either way, the paramount emotion shown is anger.

Anger, however, is not really the main culprit. It is only a secondary emotion, usually felt in response to a more primary feeling, which means that anger is more of a response than the root of the situation. Submerged under anger are four basic feelings that help define or give purpose to our rage. Chances are, if you are feeling anger, you can trace it to any of these four emotions.

Guilt
Inferiority
Fear
Trauma or pain

We have developed an acronym for these underlying emotions so you can easily trace them to their root cause. We chose the word

GIFT because we feel that it would be a GIFT to you, and to your spouse, to identify the root of your wrath. If you respond to your mate in anger, it tends to create a defensive or angry response in return. Healthy communication is thwarted, and conflict goes unresolved. By tracing the root of your anger, you may be able to share it more effectively with your mate. The GIFT Exercise gives you a format for tracing the root of your rage.

Proverbs says, "A wise man controls his anger. He knows that anger causes mistakes" (14:29) and "A gentle answer turns away wrath, but harsh words cause quarrels" (15:1). The purpose of this exercise is to help you relate your frustration, irritation, and rage more honestly. We have seen that if one partner relates in anger, the other is much less likely to really hear what he or she is saying. If, however, that same mate responds by sharing what is really wrong (that is, guilt, inferiority, fear, or pain), then the partner is much more apt to listen and change.

At first, you may resist believing that anger is really veiling these four basic feelings. But if you look further, you may be able to see the root cause of your rage. When someone cuts you off in traffic, how do you feel? You want to even the score—perhaps pull out in front of him, block his way, yell a few names, or even gesture at him. You feel disregarded, cut off, put down. Does this sound like inferiority to you? Another example may be when a relative calls and whines that you have not called her in a while. Many times you respond with defensiveness and anger, when what you really feel is guilt. Think about what makes you mad in your marriage relationship. Now look for the root. Isn't it found in your GIFT?

Levels of Anger

There are five basic levels of anger: annoyance, irritation, frustration, anger, and rage. Almost every time a couple tells us what they do not like about their marriage, one of these levels is mentioned.

1. **Annoyance.** This is the bothersome feeling you get about your partner's tedious, trifling behaviors. They are not monumental behaviors but rather persistent nuisances that are troublesome. An example may be when your spouse squeezes the toothpaste from the bottom and not the top of the tube, as you would prefer.

2. **Irritation.** This is the impatient sense you get about your partner's more aggravating habits that excite or bug you. An example is when your spouse always leaves crumbs on the counter after he or she makes a sandwich.

3. **Frustration.** This feeling of dissatisfaction is often accompanied by anxiety or depression. It is usually based on a sense that your needs are unfulfilled or problems are unresolved. An example is when your spouse is late for an appointment and does not call.

4. **Anger.** This strong feeling of displeasure or belligerence is aroused by real or supposed wrong. These feelings are usually sudden and can be accompanied by an impulse to retaliate. An example may be when your spouse does not help with the chores or yardwork after repeated requests, and you explode at him or her.

5. **Rage.** This violent furor burns within us when we feel a soul injustice has occurred. It can also be described as explosive anger, or anger out of control, often rooted in reactivity. The urge to retaliate is very strong. Rage can, however, be more passive-aggressive than explosive. Name calling or verbal abuse can be an outgrowth of rage. Having an affair can be a passive-aggressive way to act out rage.

As you can see, different levels of anger warrant different levels of emotion. It is helpful to identify the level you are feeling, so you can more accurately assess your needs in conflict. Rageful, abusive name calling for leaving crumbs on the counter may be an overreaction for such an offense. By identifying your level of anger, you can give a situation only the amount of anger it deserves. I once had a client who, in a fit of rage, yelled and screamed at her husband for putting the silverware in the wrong slot in the drawer. This type of extreme reactivity almost cost her marriage.

The Origin of Anger

We have now learned to identify our projections, the root of our anger, GIFT, and the level of anger we possess. Now we are ready to determine *why* this behavior is so troublesome for us. Determining this may also help us see why we are reacting so strongly to certain situations. For example, a behavior that starts out as an annoyance may really be felt in our psyches as a frustration or even as rage. This is where reactivity and negative soul impressions can play a part. At this time in a conflict, you need to ask yourself: *When have I ever felt this feeling before?*

If the feeling has its roots in the past, you are more likely to feel the same feelings you felt in previous situations. If, in your childhood, you were made to clean up after your younger siblings, and you felt taken advantage of or inferior, then you are very likely to have a similar response as an adult when you clean up your mate's crumbs from the counter.

The Response to Your Anger

The next step is identifying what you usually do in response to your anger. Ask yourself, What behaviors do I enact when I am feeling angry?

Do you yell and criticize? Do you withdraw and pout? Do you try to lecture and control? Chances are that whatever you did in childhood, you will do as an adult. When you had to clean up after your messy siblings, what did your anger cause you to do? Do you have the same response today in your marriage?

The Need Behind Your Anger

Behind every frustration is a desire, and behind all levels of anger there are needs. When your spouse doesn't squeeze the toothpaste tube as you would prefer, you need him to try it your way. When you are irritated that your mate leaves her crumbs on the counter, you need her to clean up after herself. When your partner is late and does not call, you need him to consider your feelings as important.

So many times in therapy, couples come in and whine about each other to the therapist. We feel like grade-school teachers on the playground where the kids are always tattling on each other. These couples spend all their energy telling us what their mate did wrong and why it is not acceptable, instead of concentrating on what they really need in the situation. Nagging, lecturing, harping, criticizing, and blaming could be reduced to a minimum if couples would just "cut to the chase" and share what they need. Unfortunately, it is typical for couples to share their irritations, annoyances, and frustrations in the negative, not the positive. When couples share frustrations with each other, they typically say things like:

"Don't do this! What's wrong with you?"

"I can't believe you are doing this again after I've told you a million times that I can't stand it when you do this!"

"You never listen! How many times do I have to tell you to stop what you are doing?"

When a wife leaves her crumbs on the counter, it is far more likely that her husband might say, "Don't do that again," rather than, "Would you please clean up after yourself?" Most people tell us that when they make nice peaceful requests, their mates do not listen. To quote one man, "I have to yell at my wife to show her I mean business." A woman once shared, "I get tired of asking my husband, because he does not take me seriously. It is not until I get angry and threaten him, that he sees my needs." The next exercise is designed to help couples deal with this type of negative sharing by learning to listen to each other and take the negative slant out of their communication.

EXERCISE 6: THE DIGGING DEEPER EXERCISE

This exercise consists of five basic steps that we have developed that will simplify the process of expressing irritation, annoyance, frustration, and anger in your relationships. We stumbled onto this tool while dealing with our own frustrations in marriage. You will be amazed at how much conflict is resolved by using this tool. To follow the steps, you need to answer the following questions.

- What is the behavior that my mate does that triggers my anger? When my mate does this _____, I feel _____.
- What is the root of my anger? (Use the GIFT Exercise.)
- When have I ever felt this feeling before?
- What do I do when I feel this feeling? What is my behavior?
- What do I really *need*?

Rob's and Laura's Digging Deeper Exercises

Rob and Laura came into therapy because their anger was destroying their relationship. They both reported that they fought almost all the time and could not resolve situations easily. Laura's main complaint was that Rob would not help her with the housework and that he criticized her jewelry business. Rob was upset because he thought the house was always a mess, and that Laura was on the phone all the time with her girlfriends, when she needed to spend more time attending to things around the house. He resented Laura's asking for help, because he felt she would not need his help if she spent less time on the phone with her friends. Laura defended herself by saying that she was selling jewelry, so why didn't he support her. These conflicts usually ended in screaming matches, with no resolution.

Rob and Laura made certain statements that triggered hurt and rage in each other. These were impact statements, spoken out of their hurt and pain, which served to wound each other even more. Their soul wounds were interactive. Rob's deepest issues interactively affected Laura's issues in a negative way and vice versa. Rob's criticism of Laura's business reminded her of the criticism she received from her family as a child. She was starting to become resentful and bitter, just as she had when she was a little girl. When Laura nagged Rob to help her with household chores, it reminded him of his mother's whining. He felt suffocated and annoyed by his wife, just as he had felt so many years ago. Rob also felt that his mother was too demanding, and he was starting to feel the same about Laura. Each was reinjuring the other and stepping right into the other's soul pain. The impact statements they made to each other were beginning to erode their marriage. By the time they came to us for marriage counseling, they were feeling a sense of doom about their relationship. After a few sessions we had them complete the Digging Deeper Exercise. Here is what they found.

Laura's Digging Deeper Exercise

1. What does my mate do that triggers my anger?
When Rob criticizes me about my business or the housework, *I feel* put down and inadequate, as if I'm not good enough, and hurt.

2. What is the root of my anger? I feel put down, and hurt, the roots are *inferiority* and *pain*.

3. When have I felt this before? As a child, when my father called me stupid and constantly ordered me to do chores but never helped me do them.

4. What was my response? To get angry, yell, and continue doing what I was criticized for. I often ignored their requests for change (passive-aggressive).

5. What did I really *need*? To be respected and affirmed for my abilities. Help with housework.

Rob's Digging Deeper Exercise

1. What does my mate do that triggers my anger?
When Laura nags me about helping her with household chores, *I feel* suffocated, and inferior, as if I can never do enough for her.

2. What is the root of my anger?
I feel taken advantage of and neglected by the time and money she spends on her dumb business. I feel suffocated and controlled by her nagging about chores, the roots being *inferiority* and *pain*.

3. When have I felt this before? When my brothers used to borrow money from me and not pay it back. My mother worked all the time, so I had to do a lot of the chores around the house. She was critical and nagged all the time. I felt inadequate; I could never do enough for her, so I wasn't good enough.

4. What was my response? I held in my frustration and eventually exploded. Then I yelled and criticized to even the score.

5. What do I really *need*? To feel appreciated and important to Laura. To be asked, not commanded, to help her with the housework. I need her to respect my feelings and ideas.

As you can see, their responses to anger worked against each other. Rob would take it until he exploded and then yell at Laura. She would yell back and then ignore his implied or verbal requests for change. They both felt misunderstood and disregarded. Their deeper feelings were inferiority and pain. As they began to work through this exercise, they could see that they were interactively tapping into each other's soul wounds. They were doing and saying the very things that would hurt their spouse the most (impact statements). It became obvious to them that their responses to anger were making things worse in their marriage.

After completing the Digging Deeper Exercise, Rob and Laura shared their results with each other in a calm, healing manner. We gave them some guidelines in this sharing. They could not interrupt, only listen until it was their turn to speak. They also had to listen with empathy. They had to practice koinonia, or hearing each other's pain as if it were their own. As they were sharing, they began to hear the deeper meaning behind each other's anger. This brought a new understanding to them. Sharing, without so much rage, helped them really listen to each other. They could hear each other's needs for the first time in their relationship. They could then work toward ways of meeting those needs in order to heal their soul wounds and to heal themselves. This couple was then ready to change their unhealthy behaviors.

Some areas are harder to discuss than others. This next chapter shares ways for couples to approach those really hard-to-discuss areas in couples communication, those areas that are particularly soul wounding. Some may even call them soul-murdering wounds that couples inflict upon each other. Next you will learn how to discuss these issues with your spouse.

Chapter 9

Communicating the Hard Stuff

The focus of this chapter is to teach you how to share the really hard stuff in marriage. It will also show you how to build forgiveness into the everyday life of your relationship. You will see how couples can learn to forgive and heal the hard-to-forgive soul wounds like adultery, abuse, and addiction that befall so many of today's marriages.

As marriage counselors, we are trained to identify the problem areas in a family system. These are the issues that many couples have difficulty discussing. These problems cause either a fight or flight response, which means the person either withdraws and shuts down, or conflicts and fights about these issues. Tom and I call these hard-to-discuss topics *Toxic Subjects*. According to Allison Bass, the five most common problem areas for couples are: sex, money, in-laws, child rearing, and roles/household chores (1–2). Irreconcilable differences centered on these topics are commonly listed as the main reasons for divorce in our society. Studies also show that there are several ways in which couples handle conflict that are proven predictors of divorce. We want to share these with you to help you prevent these dysfunctional patterns from infiltrating your marital communication. These negative behaviors can actually exacerbate marital struggles and foster even more opposition between spouses. If you find that you and your spouse have already fallen into some of these communication traps, we will show you a way out.

Predictors of Divorce

John Gottman, professor of psychology at University of Washington, Seattle, conducted a study of two hundred marital couples for ten years to examine their communication patterns. His goal was to determine what types of communication patterns destroy marriages and what types help them survive. His findings were enlightening. The number-one predictor of divorce in marriages today is *withdrawal* or *stonewalling*.

Stonewalling/Withdrawal

Stonewalling is withdrawing, or shutting down, and refusing to deal with conflict. It can be done emotionally, by closing off and refusing to talk, or physically, by walking away or leaving. Gottman found that stonewalling is typically done more by the husband. He also found that it is normative for the wife to take the emotional responsibility for the marriage. Most of the time, she is the one who brings up the thorny issues that need to be negotiated and resolved, and she is the one who persists until the discussion ends in a satisfactory resolution or in a screaming match. Gottman found that many times this can be irritating to husbands who were much less willing to bring conflict to the table. Men were more likely to ignore or live with what they considered minor disappointments than risk a big argument (Bass 3). When wives do bring up conflicting issues, husbands have a tendency to avoid or minimize them and treat them as if they are no big deal. This brings out the pursuer in the wife who is angry that her concerns are being dismissed. As a result she may maximize them and become critical, reciting a litany of what is wrong in the marriage in order to convince her husband that a serious problem exists. Thus we see the number-two predictor of divorce, which is *criticism*.

Criticism

Because men are more likely to avoid conflict, women become critical of them for minimizing issues. Wives tend to bring up difficult issues because they want certain situations to change. They usually do this by nagging their mates. Men, in turn, feel pressured and withdraw even more. We have a ready-made formula for the pursuer/distancer dyad. Like so many of the couples, they are playing a "marital Pac-Man," where one chases the other, in an effort to "chomp 'em up." Each resents the other for the patterns established.

When the wife gets upset she may resort to whining, nagging, or criticism: Why don't you? Why can't you? You never..., What's wrong with you? Unfortunately, this defeats her purpose because it creates in her husband the avoider reaction, which is the number-three predictor of divorce, known as *defensiveness.*

Defensiveness

As the pursuer (oftentimes the wife) becomes more reactive and begins to spout a litany of the wrongs in the marriage, her criticisms create a defensiveness in her husband. He becomes inflamed with the natural desire to defend himself. The more she hurls exaggerated details, the more defensive he becomes. He then starts to make excuses, lay blame, or develop some criticisms of his own: I'm only doing this because of you.

Proverbs says:

> The fool who provokes his family to anger and resentment will finally have nothing worthwhile left (11:29).

> A fool is quick tempered; a wise man stays cool when insulted (12:16).

> Self-control means controlling the tongue! A quick retort can ruin everything (13:3).

A wise woman builds her house, while a foolish woman tears her's down by her own efforts (14:1).

Criticism begets criticism, and defensiveness begets defensiveness. No one is truly being heard when this happens. Because each partner has been wounded, and attempts to heal these wounds have been unsuccessful, each person begins to build resentment and even unforgiveness toward his or her mate. Their souls no longer feel nourished and safe. Their needs are not being met as they once were. This leads to the last predictor of divorce, *contempt*.

Contempt

Since it takes twenty positive comments to make up for one "zinger" (Springle 184), you can see that couples who are in this criticism/defensiveness pattern are moving quickly downhill, in terms of building a caring, warm relationship. Some even quit. They may quit literally or emotionally, by having an affair or diving into television, work, or children. Either way, they are emotionally divorced. The pain of this behavior pattern causes contempt. All the passion and energy that once filled the relationship has now turned into a seething ember of hostility in their souls. This anger can move on the continuum from mere apathy—I don't care, I'll just do my own thing, and get my own needs met—to pure hatred—I cannot forgive my mate or trust him or her ever again. This bitterness and resentment can cause a couple to be overwhelmed with negative emotion. As a result, they have a hard time seeing anything positive in the marriage at all.

Zach and Kelly's Story

Zach and Kelly were one such couple. They came to our office as a last resort before filing for divorce. Kelly started the session by saying that she hated Zach for the things he had done in the marriage.

"For starters," she said, "he has taken the family down his shaky vocational path for the last ten years. He has spent all the equity in our house on several stupid business ventures and isn't even making much money in his business now. His irritability and temper have cut me to the quick all these years. But the final blow came when he told me he had had a brief affair with a girl at work."

"I keep trying to tell Kelly that my affair is over. It was a dumb mistake and I will never do anything like that again," Zach retorted. "She just can't leave the past in the past. She's always gotta dig everything up and throw it in my face."

Already we see the pursuer/distancer dyad at work. Kelly would cry and then blow up and scream or magnify the problems in the marriage, while Zach would get defensive and minimize his transgressions. This created a vicious cycle that usually ended in highly destructive fights. While they both began to feel defeated, Kelly was starting to feel like quitting. Apathy took the place of angst, and eventually she began to feel hatred and contempt for Zach.

Unfortunately, we do see quite a few couples like Zach and Kelly. As you can imagine, they are very challenging to work with. Sometimes we think if they had only come in sooner, it might not be so hard. But often, we are one link in a chain of therapists who have attempted to get couples to heal their marriage, but to no avail. Our first task is to try to overcome their resistance to change.

Zach and Kelly's Resistance to Change

In the previous chapter we showed you how a couple can get in touch with what is really eating them and why by completing the Digging Deeper Exercise. We shared this with Zach and Kelly, but they were so angry that they did not want the hear that the root of their anger was anything but each other.

"What do you mean dig deeper?" Kelly shrieked, "I don't have to dig any deeper than last month. You want to know the root of my anger? It's Zach! He's the cause of all this anger! It's all his fault. I don't have to dig any deeper to find that out!"

Zach, on the other hand, had a theory of his own. "You see what I gotta' deal with here? She blames me for everything! The stinkin' car breaks down, and she's gotta say it's my fault. You want to know the root of my anger? *You're lookin' at her!*"

We knew from this that it was going to be a challenge for us to get these two to stop the blame game long enough to see what was really eating them and what part they each played in their struggles. We started by inviting them to a Soul Healers Workshop. As usual, they were very skeptical. Our last resort was to appeal to their budget. They both reluctantly agreed to come after we made the point that the workshop was cheaper than paying an attorney a retainer for divorce proceedings. Besides, we told them, at least at the workshop you have a chance. Once you're in an attorney's office, you are on your way to the end. They came to the workshop balking and resistive, but they did show up. We could now get them to take a deeper look at what their soul wounds were all about. The results of the work they did are discussed in the next section.

Zach and Kelly's Digging Deeper Exercise

Step 1. We started by asking each person what his or her mate did that triggered the anger. Zach started first by saying that Kelly kept a long account of the wrongs he had done. He thought she would never forgive him or forget what he had done.

"I'm not saying that I was right in all that I did, but she will never let me live it down. I am afraid that she will make me pay for what I have done for the rest of my life! I just can't live this way! She uses this as an excuse to criticize me for everything that I do!"

We asked Zach, "How does that make you feel?" Zach took a moment and replied, "Sad, hurt, and never good enough for Kelly" [inferiority].

We then asked Kelly to share what triggered her anger at Zach. She replied, "He is selfish, and cares more for himself than for his family. He has taken us through a lot of shaky ground in regard to his many business ventures and does not even care how I feel about things. I feel as if his 'fling' was a personal slap in my face, after all my family and I have done for him!"

We asked Kelly, "How does this make you feel?" "Hurt, and unimportant, as if I am nothing to Zach and he could care less about me and the kids!" [inferiority].

As we learned in the previous chapter, anger is not the primary feeling in a given situation. Underneath anger is a GIFT that will help set you free. Step 2 of this exercise was that both Zach and Kelly had to look at what was behind their rage.

Step 2: The GIFT Exercise. We asked them to identify the roots of their anger. (Remember the roots of anger are guilt, inferiority, fear, trauma [hurt or pain]).

Zach's GIFT Exercise: Zach felt put down, constantly reminded of his sins, and unloved. The roots of his anger were *inferiority* and *guilt*.

Kelly's GIFT Exercise: Kelly felt unimportant, disregarded, as if her needs did not matter, unsafe, unprotected, uncared for, and unloved. The roots of her anger were *fear*, *hurt*, and *inferiority*.

Step 3. We asked each of them, "When in your (early) past have you felt this feeling before?"

As Zach began to examine his past, he remembered that he had felt this feeling of being put down and hurt by his mother and father. He was the middle child of three boys, and his parents had very high expectations for all of them. When he was in junior high school, his grades slipped so they took him out of sports and made him study most of the evening, while all of his friends and his brothers were playing on various teams. Zach had a difficult time with this because he loved sports and excelled there. He resented his parents for their lack of understanding, and from that point he began to rebel and get into trouble. He also never felt worthy enough or a part of anything after that. He spent most of his adult life as a Christian trying to prove that he was worthy enough. This was the same kind of pain he felt when Kelly would put him down and criticize him.

Kelly grew up in a rural farm town in the Southeast. She was the oldest of five children. Her parents were farmers, and the family always struggled for money. She started selling eggs and picking cotton for spending money when she was eleven. All through her life she carried a deep fear that she was not going to be provided for. When Zach would get one of his money-making ideas, she would feel that same fear again. When she would talk to him about it, and he would minimize her fear or ignore it. With Zach, she felt the same hurt of the little girl who was responsible for taking care of her family in those hard times.

Although Kelly described her father as a loving man, she said when times were really hard, he lost his temper and made her keep all of her siblings quiet or out of his hair, so he could watch TV or go to bed.

This feeling of pain and too much responsibility was exactly what she felt when Zach would have a "tantrum," as she called it, and tell her that he needed her help and support to be successful in his wacky business ventures.

By completing Steps 2 and 3 of this exercise, Kelly did not see an insensitive, angry adult Zach who could care less about his family. Rather, she saw a young boy who felt he could never earn his family's love and approval. Zach did not see a critical, controlling adult Kelly, but rather a frightened hurt little girl who worried about her future and feared not having enough to get along. They started seeing a wounded child's face on each other.

Step 4. We asked each of them, "What do you do when you feel this way?"

Zach said, "When I feel inferior, as if I can't do anything right, I become passive-aggressive, or I get angry and rage."

Kelly response was, "When I feel afraid for the future, I try to control and fix everything. I do this by nagging or complaining."

It is clear that the very things that Zach does infuriate Kelly and only serve to aggravate her nagging and controlling behaviors. Kelly's nagging and controlling response is just the behavior that sends Zach into a tailspin, where he is likely to become even more passive-aggressive (that is, have an affair) or become angry and rage at Kelly. This, in turn, escalates their negative cycle. The principle of interactivity is now fully operational in their relationship. They are making impact statements that hurt each other deeply. Remember, we tend to unconsciously select mates who will have issues that exacerbate ours and vice versa. It is easy to see why this couple would think that they are not good for each other. It is also easy to see why they would feel like giving up.

Step 5. Finally, we asked, "What do you really need?"

Zach identified a lifelong need for approval and validation. He needed to finally feel good enough. His short-term need was for Kelly to "give him a chance," in other words, to try to forgive him and to trust him again.

Kelly needed to feel provided for and protected by Zach. She wanted Zach not to rage at her. She wanted to feel that he cherished and loved her. She also needed him always to be faithful.

It is important to note that many people list what they need in the negative like Kelly—that Zach not rage at me anymore. We ask our clients to state their need in the positive because it is more effective in motivating human behavior. We encouraged Kelly to say—that Zach love and cherish me, and act accordingly.

Motivating individuals by the positive, not the negative, has proven to be very effective in behavior modification and motivation theory. Have you ever heard a coach say to his best pitcher, "What ever you do, don't throw an inside fast ball." What do you think the pitcher does? You guessed it! He throws the fastest inside fast ball of his career. Couples need to remember that motivating their spouse works better when they state requests in the positive, not the negative.

Our couple now knew what each other needed and why. They were just about ready to do the Behavior Change Request exercise, designed specifically to change actual behaviors in each other. (This will be further explained in Chapter 10.) But even with the insight they received from the previous exercise, they were still blocked. They still saw each other in the enemy's camp. We knew we needed an extraordinary tool that would facilitate sharing and eventually forgiveness. It would have to be an exercise designed specifically for couples traveling in a very dark place in their relationship. So we put our heads together and developed the Forgiving Experience.

EXERCISE 7: THE FORGIVING EXPERIENCE

This exercise is based on a composite of several premises that we have learned through the last twenty years. The first is from Alcoholics Anonymous. We copied a form of their Fourth and Fifth Steps, in which individuals are encouraged to take a moral inventory of the wrongs they have done and begin the process of making amends for them (Bill W. 56ff). We have adapted this, however, to include a list of what your mate has done to you that you cannot seem to forgive. The purpose of this is to clean the slate of past hurts once and for all, and move the couple toward healing.

The second premise of the Forgiving Experience is based on an exercise called the Container, which is a part of Harville Hendrix's Imago Relationship Theory. He uses this tool to enable couples to express anger and resentment to each other in a safe and constructive environment. One partner shares his anger about past wounds and hurts and the other serves as a "container" for the rage. Rather than reacting, the listener puts on her "psychic armor" and stays calm and focused, as the rage washes over her. This allows her to really hear what her mate is saying. There are two reasons for this exercise: (1) to say what hurts you, and give it the anger it deserves, and (2) to let the water "go under the bridge" (*Getting* 170–196). In other words, let the anger be expressed and resolved so you can put the past in the past, and move ahead in the relationship, unencumbered by past pain.

The last premise of the Forgiving Experience is based on the work of theologian and teacher Lewis Smedes in his work on forgiveness. In his book *Forgive and Forget*, Smedes states that for true forgiveness to occur and for trust to be rebuilt, several things have to happen. One is that the person asking for forgiveness must truly feel the pain that they have inflicted upon the other person. The partner requesting forgiveness needs to be willing to empathize with their victim. This is not an easy task because it brings up all the guilt that the perpetrator does not want to feel (50–58).

In Zach and Kelly's case, it was an arduous process. They both had a tremendous resistance to doing this exercise, but they felt it might be their last hope. Kelly planned to share first. As she began to tell Zach about her painful memories of him, his response was to empathetically put on his "psychic armor" and place himself in her shoes. He was ready to feel what Kelly felt when she experienced these injustices. It took a good deal of prayer to help Zach and Kelly with this process.

It is not just important to feel the pain we have inflicted on others, we must also make a statement to this effect. Zach's job then was to make a statement of empathy that showed Kelly that he was trying his best to understand her pain. By doing so, he allowed both of them to start experiencing koinonia. They started hearing each other's stories and feeling each other's pain as if it were happening to them, as if it were their own.

After Zach made his empathic statement, he then needed to make a statement of commitment to change his behavior. This statement is not just another empty promise that couples make after the heat of battle. It is a statement made with the full intent of one's heart and soul. At this point, Zach could not guarantee that he could change, but he could guarantee his soul intent. Promising with one's heart and soul is a sacred covenant and cannot be taken lightly.

After all of this, it is time for the final statement of amends. The perpetrator, or the listener, asks the sender, "Will you please forgive me?" The sender, we hope, grants amnesty to his or her perpetrating partner. Forgiveness is not extorted from the wounded one; it is merely requested. If the person cannot grant forgiveness at this time, he or she makes a commitment to work on the forgiveness process.

We see too often that Christians wound each other and then quickly ask for forgiveness. The person wanting forgiveness has little remorse, and the hurting person offers pardon out of guilt or duty, not from their heart and soul. Smedes calls this "forgiving without integrity." To forgive *with* integrity, both parties must thoroughly consider the crime and give it the emotional and moral energy it deserves. The purpose of forgiveness is not only to pardon the requester, but also to set the victim's soul free. Unforgiveness poisons the soul. Granting grace and absolution to a perpetrator frees the soul. But it must be done with sacredness and a reverence that ofttimes can only come from God's supernatural power. Some soul-murdering crimes can only be forgiven with God's grace.

We would like to walk you through the specific steps of the Forgiving Experience one last time, so you can get the complete picture of this process.

1. List the main (soul-wounding) hurts and resentments in your marriage.
2. Share the list with your partner. The receiver needs to be a "container" for his or her mate's rage. The sender needs to give it the anger it deserves.
3. The receiver/perpetrator feels the pain of the sender with empathy and koinonia.
4. The receiver makes an empathetic statement.
5. The receiver asks, "Will you please forgive me?"
6. The sender prayerfully grants forgiveness (as much as possible).
7. The receiver promises with the intent of his or her heart and soul to make changes in the future. Specific changes are mentioned.
8. The sender responds with gratitude or appreciation.

These eight steps may be the hardest eight steps a couple can take. We have found that if the couple will ask for help in making them, they can actually heal the bitterness and contempt that causes their souls to atrophy spiritually and relationally.

It is a sacred thing to be a part of a couple sharing from the depths of their souls. There is something awesome and completely reverent about being a catalyst for this kind of healing within a marriage. We felt this same reverence when Zach and Kelly shared their Forgiving Experience with us.

Zach and Kelly's Forgiving Experience

Kelly started by sharing about the fear and pain she had felt for their ten years of marriage, as Zach had moved the family five times and changed jobs about as often. "I have never felt safe, protected or loved by you. I lived in fear that you would go belly-up, and we would be on the street. You took too many chances with our money, especially when the kids were born." Kelly began to weep profusely. She was indeed giving it the anger and emotion it deserved. "If I tried to tell you what was troubling me, you got mad and yelled, or pouted and left. I could never tell you how I felt without you making me pay somehow. Not only did I feel that I had to be responsible to pay the bills and have some savings, but when I said no to some of your ideas, you would rage at me or punish me by closing me out. I hate you for that." Kelly was crying very hard now. Zach was doing his job as a "container," but several times he wanted to interrupt her and get defensive. We calmly encouraged him to keep his "psychic armor" on and just listen.

Kelly continued, "The final blow came for me when you had a fling with that tramp at work. I just can't believe you would ever do that. I thought you would do a lot of things, but I never thought you would stoop that low! How could you do this to me? How could you break our trust? I am so mad and hurt at you that I could scream!" Kelly's voice was now very tight and angry, instead of tearful.

She paused for a moment and then began to connect her feelings about Zach with her feeling growing up with her parents on the farm. "I feel just as I did when I was a kid and had to sell eggs to help my family out. I felt then just as I do now, that it is all up to me." At this point, Kelly started weeping from her soul. "I felt all alone when I was a kid. I had too big a burden to help the family survive. I hate feeling this way. I married you to be my helper, and I don't want to feel this way with you anymore." She then did something interesting; she expressed a huge sigh of relief. I could tell she felt lighter just by the expression on her face.

We have found this to be a common occurrence for the sender during this exercise. Giving a situation the anger it deserves can be very freeing for the soul. It tends to create a natural sense of "soul lightness" in the sender that is often accompanied by a sigh, a smile, or even laughter. We were now ready for Zach's part. He needed to make a statement of empathy to show Kelly that he could relate to her feelings.

"Kelly, that must have been awfully scary for you all those years. I had no idea all that was going on inside you. I never meant to hurt you. I didn't do those things on purpose. I really never meant to hurt you...I'm so sorry...[a long pause]...Could you ever find it in your heart to forgive me? Would you please forgive me?" (There was a reverent pause, and Kelly could see that Zach was crying softly.)

"Zach, I can't say that I can forgive you for everything yet. The affair...well, that's...that's just real hard. I can say that I will try with God's help to forgive you, but you've gotta try too. You gotta never do that stuff again."

"I won't," Zach said, waiting for his cue from us to see what he was supposed to do next. We gently instructed him to make a commitment to the future to change his behavior. "Kelly, I'll do everything I can to find out why I did those things, and I will work real hard on my temper. Bev and Tom are gonna help me. I want to be good to you and the kids. I promise I'll never screw around again...never...never!" (Zach said this as he wept quietly.)

This is where God's awesome healing power takes over. This is where we as therapists feel that we are on holy ground. As Zach sat there crying in angst, his angry, hurting wife, his intimate enemy, the woman who declared absolute contempt for him, reached out and gently took his hand. This was the beginning of their peacemaking. They looked into each other's eyes and started to cry, then spontaneously hugged each other as an outgrowth of the goodwill they felt at that moment. This is such a sacred time for couples, that many times we just leave the room, and let God's healing power engulf them. Even though as therapists, we have seen this many times, we were crying too with this couple.

This exercise was a real breakthrough for Zach and Kelly. It did not solve all of their problems, but it did redirect them on a road toward healing. They rebuilt their friendship and are now working very hard to build trust in each other and become soul healers. For them to do this however, they have to begin to change some of their dysfunctional behaviors. The next chapter is dedicated to behavior change, which is a strategic part of becoming soul-healing partners.

Chapter 10

If Nothing Changes, Nothing Changes

Perhaps the hardest job of a therapist is to be a catalyst of behavior change. For most couples, the change process is much like Zach and Kelly's story. They fall in the same holes in the sidewalk of marital conflict and have a very difficult time getting out. Gaining insight into why they do what they do can be very beneficial for many people. But if their dysfunctional behavior does not change, this insight can be seemingly useless. After all, change is what is desired in therapy, isn't it? Change is the therapeutic bottom line. Couples want to know what is going to be different. They ask how their unhealthy behavior patterns can be altered?

What can they expect to be modified? However, change can be very difficult for couples. In this chapter we are going to examine couples' resistance to the change process, and what can be done about it.

Couples often come into the counseling process fraught with fear that the system will not be any different. This can create not only resistance to the change process but can also sabotage any relationship modification. Sometimes one partner may change, and the other does not even notice. Fear can blind a person to his or her mate's attempts toward healing. Many partners say, "I'll change only after my mate changes." Neither mate wants to be vulnerable, or take a risk, until there is some goodwill gesture on behalf of the partner. These couples spend a great deal of time and energy in therapy resisting the change process, rather than working toward healing. Frequently made statements include:

He's been like this for thirty years. He'll never do anything different.

I'll have to do all the changing.

I changed, and she didn't even notice.

You can't teach an old husband new tricks. He is just set in his ways.

If I had money for every time I asked my mate to change, I'd be rich by now.

She'll change for a little while, but soon she'll go back to her old ways.

These couples are steeped in fear and pain, fear that the system will never change and pain from soul wounds that life and marriage have inflicted upon them. Some have even stopped praying for their mate and for their marriage. We see couples like these come in with all levels of hopelessness, from tiresome frustration to apathy, to actually living in an emotional divorce. Our goal is to bring about change, but first we have to rebuild the couple's faith.

Faith As a Resource for Change

Christian couples have the infinite resources of God Almighty at their fingertips, yet when they get scared, they seem to forget this. Their fear and pain block God's healing power from reaching their souls. The daily grind of life and a difficult marriage cause it to fade from the horizon. These couples strongly desire their marriage to change, yet they continue in the same dysfunctional behaviors. Patricia Love, author and Imago Therapy trainer, has a saying: "If nothing changes, nothing changes."[1] This reminds me of John

Bradshaw's definition of insanity: "Insanity is doing the same thing over and over again and expecting different results."[2] This is, in fact, what most couples do. They repeat the same unhealthy patterns over and over again, while expecting things to be different. These couples need to apply their faith in God's supernatural healing power to bring about behavior change in their marriages. They also need to take a look at their own behaviors, and if they are not working, change them!

Resistance to Change

For couples to do this, they need to overcome the barriers or resistance. Motivational speaker Denis Waitley says that there are two basic human motivators: fear and desire (32ff). These emotions motivate humankind to change. We know that troubled couples have the desire to change or they would not be coming to therapy. We are then left with only one reason they are not acting on their desire—their fear is too great.

To bring about change, we need to find out why that fear is there and then begin to exorcise it. This fear manifests itself in several forms, all of which cause resistance to the change process. By sharing several of the reasons couples resist change, we can show people how to allow God's healing power to overcome their reluctance to become healthy. The next sections discuss forms of fear.

Hurt

Many of the couples we see say they really want to live as soul mates. They hear sermons and Sunday school lectures on God's plan for intimacy between man and wife, but they are frustrated because they cannot seem to cultivate these fruits in their own life. Most of the time, their resistance is rooted in the hurt and pain that they have experienced in the past. These individuals feel so hurt that they cannot ever picture being friends, much less soul mates, with their partner. Healing their hurt is essential if they are going to try to become soul healers.

Fear of the Unknown

Even though their relationship may be unhealthy, some couples resist change because it is unknown. The familiar seems better than that which they have not yet experienced. The book of Exodus shows us the historical example of the children of Israel who stayed in captivity rather than risk the change that would bring about freedom. Their fear of the unknown held them back from the Lord's blessings. Many fearful couples can learn from this example.

Feeling Uncomfortable with or Unworthy of Happiness

Sometimes resistance to change can be traced to an unconscious feeling that you do not deserve to be happy. If you did not get your needs met as a child, or your parents modeled an unhappy marriage, you may unconsciously feel as if you should not have fulfillment or happiness as well. This may not be an overt feeling, but you may have developed many covert ways to sabotage your marital satisfaction. You may unconsciously feel guilty if you are happy and find ways to ruin or sabotage it.

The exercises in the previous chapter can be very helpful in healing many of these areas. They can also motivate the couple to move through their resistance to the change process. The Soul Healogram can uncover any unconscious feelings of guilt about being happily married. The Digging Deeper Exercise can unearth any sabotage patterns that may cause you to resist behavior change. The Forgiving Experience can help heal previous hurts you or your mate have inflicted upon each other, so you are both free to make the changes necessary to become soul healers.

This next exercise is designed specifically to heal problematic behaviors. It is designed to bring simplicity and clarity to the change process, so change can be viewed as feasible and plausible. Dr. Harville Hendrix aptly named this exercise the Behavior Change Request (*Keeping* 288–91).

EXERCISE 8: THE BEHAVIOR CHANGE REQUEST

Here is how it works. When irritation, annoyance, frustration or anger occur in a relationship, you can use the GIFT Exercise to determine the root feeling. From this technique, you are also able to clearly define your needs. You will notice from previous chapters that people define their needs in a very broad or general sense. We hear generalized statements like "I just want him to love me more," or "I want her to respect me." Although the goal is not stated in the negative, it is still much too broad. It is harder to accomplish goals that are too broad or too general. The more specific a goal is, the greater likelihood it can be achieved. Therefore, couples need to state their goals in very specific terms. Dr. Harville Hendrix says that needs are more likely to be met if they are doable, measurable, and quantifiable (*Keeping* 290). *Doable* means that the goals are achievable or realistic. *Measurable* means that progress in meeting these goals can be ascertained, or that an estimate of what has been completed can be determined. And finally, *quantifiable* means that the quantity and frequency of the behaviors can be determined (that is, when and how many times). The ability for couples to measure their progress helps them in the change process. It shows them their own progress, as well as their mate's. It also helps them see God's hand in the healing of their marriage. The Behavior Change Request provides couples with a tool to make behavioral goals more realistic and achievable.

To complete this exercise, you first need to state the needs you ascertained from the GIFT Exercise. List each need on a sheet of paper entitled *Behavior Change Request*. Under each need, write three specific behaviors that will meet that need. For example, if you are angry and hurt with your spouse, and you complete the GIFT Exercise and determine that you need more help and support, you will then need to list this need for help and support in the form of specific behaviors. Your BCR or Behavior Change Request would look like this:

Behavior Change Request

Needs:
Support and help with household chores

Behaviors:
1. I would like for my mate to cook supper one night per week. This will start this week.

2. I would like for my mate to bathe the kids two nights per week. This will start next week.

3. I want my mate to listen to me talk about work and later bring up various things that I have discussed. This will start this week.

4. I desire that my mate compliment my vocational abilities at least once every week. This will commence this week.

You can see these goals are realistic and measurable. The frequency is specified so they are also quantifiable. There is a starting time, which takes the anxiety out of wondering when one's mate will actually complete the desired requests. This also provides a means for the mate to "get credit" for the changes he or she has made.

Often, one mate will make a few changes, but they will go unnoticed because there is no means by which to measure their progress. This can be very discouraging for the partner trying to change. It can even cause them to want to give up. The BCR takes the guesswork out of the couple's change process. It actually gives couples a road map to follow in healing their relationship.

But Why Do I Have to Ask?

Perhaps one of the greatest hurdles to overcome in completing the BCR is the feeling that the changes made are really shallow, phony, or contrived. Many people still believe the myth that "if someone really loves you they can read your mind." Therefore, they will know your need without you having to ask. As therapists, we hear things:

> If I have to spell out change, it is not from the heart.

> Why do I have to tell him what I want and need?

> If he really loved me, he would just know.

> She's only making these changes because I asked her to. Since it was not her idea, she doesn't mean it.

> If I have to ask my husband to give me what I need, the gift looses its specialness.

> My mate is only doing this because the therapist said to do it.

All of these feelings are natural in the change process, but we have to face them head-on in order to overcome our objections to healing. Janet Woititz, in her book *Struggle for Intimacy*, says that one of the common false beliefs about intimacy is "If you really love me, you could read my mind" (17). There are several reasons we have this false belief. One is phenylethylamine, the biochemical reaction that occurs when we fall in love (see Chapter 6). The presence of these "amphetamines" actually creates an altered state of consciousness. Many times PEA can be referred to as the "bonding chemical" because it helps you bond by enabling you to be totally tuned into your mate. You hang on her every word. You finish his sentences. He rubs his head in pain, and you are there with two aspirin to remedy him. Your prospective spouse may grab her lower back and wince in pain, and you offer a back rub. You secretly find out that she likes a particular type of flower, and you put them on her front porch, with a note that romantically intones, "Just because it is Tuesday." You and your partner do all of this for each other without either of you having to ask. All of these behaviors lead you to the extremely misleading conclusion that your partner can read your mind. This is one of the reasons you love him or her so much. Getting your needs met, without even asking, is a wonderful blessing, especially if you grew up in a home where it was not all right to ask for anything.

You suffer from the delusion (or brain chemistry) that your partner is telepathic and knows your needs and strongly desires to meet them. So when the power struggle begins, when the honeymoon is over, you believe that he or she knows your needs but does not desire to meet them any more. This is where you make up all sorts of motives about your partner:

> He just does not love me enough to meet my needs.

> She tricked me when we first met by being so caring in the beginning of our relationship. Then she started cooling off.

> He is just a selfish jerk, who cares more about himself than me and my needs.

None of these are completely true. However, they are steeped in fantasy and delusion just like the notion of your mate's marvelous mind-reading ability. The truth is that most people are not telepathic or psychic. They may get lucky with the help of certain brain chemicals, but they truly cannot read minds. The whole mind-reading notion can be put peacefully to rest if couples would just remember this premise: "The likelihood of your needs getting met increases proportionately with your ability to *ask for them out loud*." It has been substantiated through research on relationships that one's needs are met in proportion to one's asking.

But What If I Don't Have any Needs?

There are two types of people who have trouble stating their needs. The first kind is what we refer to as the "needless." These individuals are usually in fields of study that require a well-developed left brain. Thus, they are extremely rational and logical and can be very unemotional. Because of this, they see themselves as very strong and rarely focus on their psychic or soul needs. These individuals usually choose professions that require a great deal of left-brain logic. They may be engineers, scientists, chemists, lawyers, or doctors.

Then there are those who have trouble sharing their needs because they have been trained not to do so. Many of them grew up in homes where they were told it was either wrong or selfish to share their needs. Some people's needs were merely ignored or unrecognized by their family, so they stopped stating them. These people have needs, but deny them. They ask for little in a relationship, but tend to expect their partners to give to them without their having to ask. Thus, the notion of marital mind reading is born.

Darren and Samantha's Story

Darren was a trauma surgeon. He was used to putting his needs aside for the good of others. Working long hours in the ER with little sleep had become a way of life for him. Samantha was a writer for a local magazine. She was used to expressing herself, needs and all. They came into the counseling center at Sam's initiative because she felt that she wanted more out of marriage and was not happy with their current situation. I asked them what they wanted to see different in their marriage? Samantha, who was gifted with articulation and a good command of words, eloquently and thoroughly listed six things right off:

1. "That Darren share more of his feelings with me."
2. "That Darren listen more to my feelings."
3. "That Darren show interest in reading my articles."
4. "That Darren spend more time with me and the kids."
5. "That Darren share his spiritual side with me and listen to me share mine."
6. "That Darren and I become soul mates and share each other's internal world."

It was obvious that Samantha had no trouble being aware of her needs, feeling her needs, and sharing her needs. It is no surprise that she would be attracted to her opposite, Darren, who had only one need: "That Samantha not have so many needs!!"

They definitely had a problem in their relationship. To determine the root, we had to look deeper into Darren's life to see where he learned his self-denial and seeming needlessness.

Darren was raised in a loving Christian home. He described his parents as "pillars of the church." His dad was also a trauma surgeon and worked long hours. Dad was a very active community servant and spent a week every year in medical service in a Third World country. Darren's dad was a loving and warm man and an excellent example of selflessness. Darren loved his dad and wanted to be just like him. I once asked him what he thought his dad wanted and needed most out of life. He was baffled. He did not have a clue. "My dad never had needs," he sighed. "At least, he never shared them." At that moment the "idea light bulb" went off in Darren's head. He suddenly realized that he was following his father's example. He had repressed his needs just as his father had. His dad taught him well how to push his own needs down in order to attend to the needs of others. Darren feared that by sharing his needs, he would be perceived as selfish or self-absorbed. This realization was wonderful for him, because it allowed him to start recognizing what was really going on inside him.

Samantha lovingly and gently shared with Darren her excitement that he finally recognized he had needs.

"For so long, I thought something was wrong with me," Samantha exclaimed. "I thought I was terribly needy and that Darren was the strong one. I never felt that he needed me for anything. For years he made me feel useless in our relationship."

Samantha warmly invited Darren to share his needs with her. She encouraged his vulnerability and shared her own. As Darren began to state his wants and needs with his wife, the two became closer.

He was surprised and pleased as he shared, "What a paradox! I always thought that denying my needs would make me a noble and good husband. Now the wonderful truth is that by sharing that I have needs, I get a chance to heal myself, and my wife feels even closer to me than ever before. She actually likes me better this way!"

The bottom line is that Darren learned that it is normal to need. Once he began to share his needs with Sam, it was not so difficult for them to complete the Behavior Change Request. Now both Darren and Samantha can ask for and receive what they want in the marriage. Both are grateful for having the BCR as a tool to make this happen.

EXERCISE 9: MIRRORING OR PARROTING

When you are doing a BCR, it is important to really listen to your mate's requests. To assure this, it is best to give your mate direct feedback, word for word. Some relational theorists call this process *mirroring*, while some call it *active listening*, or *parroting*.[3] No matter what term is used, the result is much like the mimic game we played as children to annoy our younger siblings and peers. I can still hear my younger brother's frustrated whine as he pleaded with me to stop repeating every word he said.

Although this may have been annoying to you as a child, you will learn that it can be very helpful for you as a grown married person. You will be surprised how you or your mate can have trouble listening to even simple requests and feeding them back.

Tom and I were in class to become certified Imago therapists, and our assignment was to pair up with a fellow classmate and mirror what they were saying. I must say that I did great! I mirrored the voice inflection, pitch, tone, body language, and even restated the phrases word for word. I thought I had really mastered this technique. Then, it was my turn to mirror Tom. As he started sharing some of his frustrations with our marriage, I couldn't believe how hard it was for me to parrot him. I had trouble concentrating. I wanted to minimize or dismiss his concerns. I felt defensive and hurt and wanted to fight back or interrupt him. All of these reactions kept me from really hearing what he had to say. I was amazed at how hard it was to be a calm reflective mirror when my own reputation as a partner was at stake. Becoming a true mirror was very hard for me. The hotter the issue, the harder it was for me to truly reflect Tom's feelings. I realized then why mirroring was so important in the change process with couples. Without this tool, it is too hard for most couples to hear what each other is saying, especially when it shines a negative light. This process of mirroring makes it possible for couples to hear each other and even show each other that they are doing so.

EXERCISE 8: THE BEHAVIOR CHANGE REQUEST (CONTINUED)

Now we are ready for the next step of the BCR. Your mate states one of the three requests on his or her list and you repeat it back verbatim. In other words, you mirror the request. The only question you can ask is, "Did I get that right?" If you did not, then repeat the request until you do get it right. This may be hard at first, but give it time. You will both need to be patient because this will be new for you. Have your mate repeat all three requests, and follow the procedure for mirroring them. After each request is stated and mirrored, you may then agree to one, two, or all three of them. You will also state a time in which these requests can realistically be granted.

Let's say that your mate requests that you help more with the housework, and he suggests that you wash the dishes at least two nights per week. After you have mirrored this request, and you are sure you have heard your partner correctly, you then make an agreement to grant this request. Remember, you can only promise to do what is realistic in a time frame that is plausible. If you are going to be traveling away from home all next week, that is not the time to grant this request. You will want to save this for a week when it can be properly granted. The goal is not to have couples make grandiose promises that cannot be fulfilled. While the intent may be noble, the follow-through may be deadly. Empty promises can cause even greater pain in an already stressed marital relationship. This needs to be avoided as much as possible.

When you agree to a request from your partner, you are simply granting these petitions with no strings attached. You are not making deals with your spouse, or worrying about what you are going to get out of this. You do not grant your mate's wishes so that he or she will grant yours. This is not a quid pro quo or tit-for-tat interaction. The goal is not to give so you can get, nor to do for them so they can come through for you. The goal is to give freely, with no ulterior motives. You give your mate a present. *Webster's Dictionary* says a *present* is "a thing that is furnished or endowed as a gift." This gift, or present, is given unconditionally. It is offered as absolute, not subject to any conditions on the part of the giver. What you give to your partner is really *agape*. Does this term sound familiar to you?

Agape

Agape, which was discussed earlier, is the Greek term found in Scripture meaning "benevolence or charity, undeserved favor." It is listed as the highest form of love. When given, it is not dependent upon the worth or value of the receiver. When expressed, it carries no obligation. Agape is favor given with no requirements or conditions.

Hendrix views agape as an act of directing Eros, or life energy, away from ourselves and toward the welfare of another. He says, "In that sense it is sacrificial, but what is sacrificed is not self, but rather our preoccupation with self. Agape used as a noun denotes attitude, as a verb it denotes action towards another" (*Getting* 290ff).

Christ's Example of Agape

It is against our human nature to give unconditionally. We humans tend to give to get. Christ's directive to love our enemies and bless those that hurt us, to turn the other cheek, goes against our very structure. How can we care for those who do not care about us? How indeed, can we care for our mates when we perceive them as uncaring, or even enemies? This is where we need God's divine help. We need to call on his unconditionally loving nature to enable us to actualize that part of ourselves that is the most Christ-like. Christ then becomes the inspiration for us to transcend our humanity and follow his example. The solution to our human condition in marriage is simple. It is to love our mate as Christ first loved us. Remember, it is simple, not easy. Even with Christ's loving example to guide us, it is still hard for most Christian couples to move beyond the typical deal-making, tit-for-tat marriages that we are so used to.

> Most marriages run like a commodities market with loving behaviors as the coin in trade. This doesn't set well with the the old brain. If John rubs Martha's shoulders in hopes that she will let him go fishing the next morning, a built-in sensor goes off in Martha's head that says, 'Look out! Price tag attached'. There is no reason then for her to feel good about the gift, because she knows that she will have to pay later. She unconsciously rejects John's attentions and affections, because the only kind of love the old brain will receive is the kind with

no strings attached. This need for unconditional love comes straight from childhood. When we were infants, love came without a price tag. We did not have to reciprocate when we were patted, rocked, or fed. Now that we are adults, the old brain still craves this kind of unconditional giving. We want to be loved and cared about without doing anything in return. When our partners grant us caring loving behaviors regardless of what we do, we feel the familiar warmth, comfort, and security of our childhood (Hendrix, *Getting* 123–125).

By giving our partner presents, with no strings attached, we are healing not only their old brain but also their soul wounds. We can give these presents freely because Christ freely gave his love to us. Thus, we give to our partner because Christ gave himself to us.

Agape in Action

For years as marital and family therapists, Tom and I worked with couples to help them gain insight and then make deals. We were both trained that if couples gained enough awareness and made enough trades, they would one day feel safe in marriage. We now believe that couples do not heal their souls by deal making or insight. The wounds of soul are healed by repetition, the old brain experiencing presents, given repeatedly and consistently, as well as freely and unconditionally, by their partner.

We learned this valuable lesson after attending a couples retreat several years ago. We were asked to make a list of things that our mate could do that would make us feel secure and loved. I put on my list that I would feel warm and loved by Tom if he would serve me a cup of coffee in bed every morning, when I woke up. This was particularly meaningful to me because I felt that I was not nurtured much in this way as a child. He gladly agreed and diligently brought coffee to me every day for about a week. To be honest, I thought he was only bringing it because it was on my list. Not only did I doubt his sincerity, but I also doubted he would continue. (See what kind of tricks your old brain can play on you.)

About two weeks after we started this process of giving unconditional presents to each other, we had a spat. I am sad to admit that when we went to bed, we *did* let the sun go down on our anger. When he awoke the next morning, Tom was still perturbed and frustrated, and indeed doubted if I was deserving of his present, but he gave it anyway, because of the promises we had made to each other. He was doing his best to act with intentionality. He was "faking it till he made it." It was still hard for him to act so intentionally in the midst of his frustration. I could tell because he sloshed the cup of coffee on my night table and spilled some of it. When I saw the cup of coffee still sitting there amidst his anger and frustration, I was overwhelmed. I was overcome with emotion. I was weeping from my gut. I was crying soul tears. He felt terrible and immediately ran in to apologize.

"I'm sorry if I damaged your night stand. I can fix it," he consoled. "Please don't cry. It isn't that bad a spill."

"No," I said, gasping to catch my breath, "I'm not crying about the night stand, I'm crying because for the first time in my life since I can remember, someone was angry with me and still acted loving anyway. I'm crying because, even though you were frustrated and aggravated with me, you kept your promise to act loving toward me." He and I had a few sacred moments of crying together, as we shared the awe and wonder of healing the old brain by *the Giving of Presents*. The tears that I shed were the tears of a child who finally felt unconditionally loved (agaped), no matter what. Our souls melted into each other, and we got a little closer by sharing that special time together. It has been several years since that day, and I still get my soul-healing cup of coffee every morning. We are still awed by this vivid example in our own marriage of the power of the Giving of Presents in the healing of our old brain, as well as our souls. As you, with God's help, agree to give presents to your mate, you can truly become a soul healer.

EXERCISE 10: THE GIVING OF PRESENTS

To complete this exercise, each of you needs to make a list of behaviors that would express agape to you. The list would read as follows: *I feel warm and loved by you when you...*

Fill in the list with soul presents that you would like to receive. Exchange lists, and each pick one present that you are willing to give. Bestow it on your spouse within a three-day period. The lists can be updated regularly. Remember, this is not a time to extort or test your partner. Don't list things like moving away from your in-laws, or buying a bigger house. These are soul-healing presents we are talking about here, not deals to be made, or "proof" of love. One further note: It is imperative that the presents be given consistently and as soon as possible. Do not resolve to give a present if you know you can't or won't follow through. It would have been even more damaging to my soul if Tom had brought me coffee for several weeks and then faded in his efforts. The Giving of Presents is a sacred covenant that must be done consistently and reverently.

Putting It All Together — The Behavior Change Request

In closing this chapter, we will put all the steps of the BCR together so that you can see, from start to finish, how to complete this exercise.

1. Identify your need. Use the GIFT Exercise if you need to.

2. State your needs in the form of three behavioral requests. Make sure the requests are doable, measurable, and quantifiable. Give a starting date.

3. Have your mate mirror or repeat each request, asking only if his or her mirror is accurate: "Did I get that right?" or "Is there more you want to say?"

4. Have your partner agree to one, two, or all three of the requests, stating the time that they will be completed.

5. Consistently follow through on your partner's requests.

In this chapter we have seen that the consistent, sacred, unconditional giving of soul-healing presents can heal the old brain and form a lasting bond between husband and wives. This act of giving soul-healing presents replicates God's unconditional love for us. This idea of agape is really his idea and his design for couples. The next chapter discusses in detail what God has in mind for a Christian marriage.

Chapter 11

Soul-Healing Love Is God's Idea

We see so many couples in counseling who are merely existing in their marriages. Some have tasted a small sampling of soul-healing love during the romantic stage, only to quickly watch it fade away as they slide full force into the power struggle. Some even less-fortunate couples have actually forgotten any semblance of the chemistry, passion, and caring that brought them together in the first place. In previous chapters, we have shared remedies to these relational maladies. But perhaps one of the biggest obstacles we have to overcome in the healing of relationships, is the false belief that soul-healing love does not really exist. These lonely travelers on the road of relationships have almost given up on finding the love of their life. Here are a few examples of these weary travelers.

Herman, the Not-So-Confirmed Bachelor

There was Herman, a thirty-nine-year-old rich, handsome bachelor, who came to see us because he wondered if he would ever find the "perfect girl." He dated super-models and corporate executives, who made six-figure incomes, and still he became disillusioned about finding his soul mate. We told him the problem was not that he had failed to find his soul mate; the problem was that he had not found the "soul mater" within himself. He had not yet learned to love with a soul-healing love. Learning to love in this fashion is not a mystical ability; it is a skill that is to be ascertained, honed, and practiced.

"You mean that I haven't overlooked my soul mate? You mean she may still be out there somewhere? Do you think it's possible that she hasn't married somebody else and had three kids by now?" Herman blurted out.

"No, indeed," we told him, "your soul mate will appear when you have learned to become a soul-healing partner. What has been missing in your past relationships was *you*."

Herman's quest for the perfect soul mate had kept him from learning the skills he needed within himself to be soul-healing lover.

Oliver and Lisa, the Married Skeptics

Oliver and his wife of six years, Lisa, were told by family and friends that marriage was to be endured, and that was all one could expect. Lisa wanted more. She wanted a soul mate. People told her that this did not exist. Her grandmother told her she could expect some of this soul mate "nonsense" during the courtship (maybe Grandma knew a little about phenylethylamine), but once the honeymoon was over, Lisa would just have to "settle for what she got!" To top this off, Grandma added, "and it is God's will that you never divorce." This left Lisa and Oliver feeling more as if they were being sentenced to a jail term than committing to matrimony. Lisa was particularly disillusioned at the notion of making due in marriage. She had almost given up hope that true soul-healing love was possible when she heard us speak to her church group. Our lessons gave Lisa some hope, but Oliver still remained a skeptic.

"This soul-healing stuff just isn't for me," he'd tell Lisa, refusing to darken the doors of a counseling office. "Who says this really even exists?" he would lament.

Lisa tried numerous times to convince Oliver that this kind of love was possible, but he adamantly resisted her attempts. She started feeling as if she was putting Oliver through too much. She worried that she was being almost cruel to him by trying to change him to meet her needs.

"Isn't this too much to ask of your mate?" she questioned. "What if I just picked a man who cannot do this? What if I am asking Oliver to do something that is impossible for him? What if I picked the wrong mate and my soul mate is still out there somewhere?"

It did not help her angst and guilt when Oliver acted as if Lisa was torturing him by asking him to come to marriage counseling. What Lisa did not realize was that she would not be hurting or tormenting Oliver, she would actually be healing him by asking him to change. Oliver, like all humans, was created by God to soul mate. God intended for all of us to build oneness of souls with another human being. God's plan is that we find a lifetime partner and learn to merge our soul with their soul. This union creates a soul-healing bond. Every soul needs this healing. Every soul needs to learn to love in this manner. By acquiring this awesome ability, we are actualizing our full spiritual potential, which makes the heart of God dance. God's love for each of us heals our souls, and God wants us to replicate this kind of love with our lifetime partner. By doing this, we will become more Christ-like, which is the aim of all Christians. God created all of his children to love and be loved, even Oliver.

Each time Lisa asked Oliver to come to counseling with her, and he vehemently refused, she noticed that he acted better toward her. He came home earlier, sent her flowers, or offered to do the dishes. He thought that this would change Lisa's opinion that their marriage needed help. Later when she brought up counseling again, he would become defensive and shout, "I can't believe that you still want to see a counselor, after all the changes I have made. You just want too much. I can never do enough for you. Why do you keep trying to change me?" Oliver's fear and resistance to change were overtaking him. He, like many Christians, thought counseling was for crazy couples who yelled and screamed and hated each other. He told Lisa repeatedly, "I don't see why two perfectly healthy Christian adults cannot work out their problems on their own." We have heard this prideful attitude from Christians so many times. The sad thing is that while this pride may prohibit them from going to a counselor's office, this same pride just may carry or even push them into the divorce attorney's office. This is such a sad plight for Christian couples.

Our goal quickly became to coach Lisa on how to get Oliver to come to marriage counseling. We encouraged her to share this story with him: If you had a cyst on your arm that was full of germs, you could go to the drugstore and buy some Bactine and a bandage and apply it to the lump, in hopes that the infection would abate. It may go away with this course of treatment, but in all likelihood the germs will thrive, and the cyst will begin to swell even more. When this happens, you will feel pain. You could choose to apply Bactine again, but the wiser choice would be to see a doctor. If you resist seeing a professional, the infection could become acute and you could even lose your arm.

This is what you, Oliver (and many other resistive spouses), are doing when you try to cure the infection of your marital problems with the simple Bactine of bettering surface behaviors. Your marriage needs the antibiotic of marriage counseling. You need a marriage doctor. You may even need to lance that matrimonial commitment, so the pus of negative energy and contempt can drain properly. Resisting the help that is available could be deadly for you and your marriage.

The story worked, and Oliver agreed to come to marriage counseling. It took a while for him to overcome the feeling that he was being tortured by having to learn to be a more feeling person. He and Lisa came to several Soul Healers Workshops, and in time, Oliver began to believe that soul-healing love was possible. He even started to see that it wasn't torment or punishment for the average testosterone-loaded male to learn to share his feelings and become a good communicator and listener. During their last workshop, Oliver blessed us all by openly thanking his wife for pushing him to come to marriage counseling.

We all cried as he tearfully shared: "No one was more resistant to coming to counseling than me. I was a true skeptic. I equated marriage counseling with having a root canal! I had no desire whatsoever to look at my childhood. I guess I was just scared. I have had a change of heart, however, and I want to thank my wife for fussing, begging, pushing, and pulling me to come. [At this point, Oliver could not hold back his tears, nor could we.] In my whole life, I never thought that this kind of love was possible. I guess it was because my parents have been in a miserable marriage for forty-five years. But things are different now. My wife is my best friend, and our relationship just keeps getting better and better. I want to say to all the husbands in the group that you can have this too. Thanks, honey, for not giving up on me. Thanks,

Bev and Tom, for being our marital tour guides and for teaching us the tools of soul-healing love. I feel as if all of the hard work is worth it."

Imagine all of this from a guy who initially refused to come to therapy. Oliver was and is one of our best advertisements for soul-healing love. He still sends his friends, family, and church members to our office for counseling. As you can see, Oliver and Lisa's growth had a precious, sacred impact on us all.

The Thread of Love

So how do we achieve this soul-healing love? Let's look at the various types or meanings of love as a clue to the single thread that runs through our marriage. When couples meet, they feel Eros, or romantic love. We have shown you that this love is delusional and has a very self-indulgent quality. The theories of chemistry, Imago, and projection in Chapter 6 reveal that you are attracted to someone who makes you feel good about yourself. Thus, you love someone because he or she can meet your needs. In actuality, you love the person because of what he or she can do for you. Since your needs are met, you have a false sense of euphoria and are more willing to meet the needs of your partner. However, this motivation is still somewhat selfish and self-serving.

As the power struggle starts, and your needs are not being met, you do not feel like giving. You even want to withhold and sometimes seek revenge or retaliation for the pain you feel. It is then that you must practice unconditional, undeserved favor and love. It is when you least feel like it that you need to extend agape to your partner.

I once heard, "In order to be truly safe, you must insure the safety of your enemies." Harville Hendrix amplified this saying, "True peace—that is, peace without fear—exists only among friends.

Peace with fear can exist between foes, but it is always unstable" (*Getting* 291).

To insure peace and safety between you and your partner, you must be willing to insure the peace and safety of each other. Because the power struggle has made you enemies, this peace will indeed be unstable. To bring stability to your relationship, you both must be willing to extend agape to each other. By giving your partner undeserved favor, you are extending the hand of friendship to your enemy. This act of goodwill causes a bond of friendship to form. Thus *philia*, or friendship, is born in your relationship. You and your spouse become friends.

The sequence of love moves from Eros to agape to philia. You fall in love with delusional Eros driving you and become intimate enemies, because of your own human nature and power struggles. Then, as an act of your will you learn to give agape and gradually you and your spouse become friends. So is this where love arrives? Is this the culmination of love in a long-term marriage—friendship—philia? Wow, what a simple not-so-exciting goal! At first as therapists, we were disappointed that love's destiny ended so simply and was seemingly commonplace.

Our confusion and disappointment led us to interview couples who have been happily married for over forty years to find out what they would consider the primary advantage or benefit of long-term love. We were surprised at what we found. Without exception, all of the couples pointed to friendship. In one way or another, their comments indicated friendship as the key to fulfillment in a long-term, healthy love relationship. Tom and I were expecting something more exciting like passion, mind melding, or mutual spiritual nirvana. Instead we heard pure and simple friendship (philia). Here is a sampling of what they said:

Greg and Vera, married forty-two years: "She is my best friend and I would never do anything to hurt her." "I care so much for him; if he hurts, I hurt too."

Linda and Rick, married forty-five years: "We care for one another. We really care how the other one is feeling."

Al and Murial, married forty-seven years: "The best advice we can give to young couples is—Be ye kind one to another."

Robert and Mary, married fifty-seven years: "I can't imagine life without him. He is one of the few true friends I have. I wouldn't take anything for the friendship we have developed over our lifetime. We are truly blessed."

Virgie and Harland, married sixty years: "She is my companion and my best friend in the whole world. I am so grateful to God for giving her to me."

I still remember talking with this pleasant couple about their marriage. As we were sharing, Harland left the room for a moment. Without blinking, Virgie said, "Bring me one, too."

"Bring me what?" I asked. Before Virgie could answer me, Harland walked in the room with two glasses of iced tea. "Here you are, Darlin', your tea, just like you asked for it."

"Thank you, Dear," she replied sweetly.

"Wait a minute," I said to Harland. "Virgie didn't ask for anything. How did you know what she wanted? She just said 'bring me one too' as you left the room."

They both looked at me puzzled and Harland asked, "Didn't she ask for that tea? I could have sworn she asked."

"No," I said, "she didn't say a word."

As they both began to chuckle, Harland calmly replied, "Oh well, I guess we were reading each other's minds again! We do this all the time now. We communicate so well, I guess we forget to use words." Harland continued in an almost professorial fashion, "We tell our grown kids that this mind-reading stuff doesn't come easy. They've got to learn it like Mom and I did. We didn't always know what each other wanted, we had to get it by watchin', and just bein' around each other. We got it by carin'. You just can't start off like this; it takes years to develop."

I felt privileged to be a part of that sacred moment between these long-term soul healers. It gave me hope for the future of marriage in today's times.

What we heard in our interviews is validated in Jeanette Lauer and Robert Lauer's article, "Marriages Made to Last," which gives the results of a research project that focused on happy couples. The item that all couples ranked first was "we are each other's best friend." The study showed that friendship was the most significant factor in healthy, happy, long-term couples, winning over mutual political beliefs, similar financial styles, passion, and sexual fulfillment (85–89).

To attain this friendship, we humans have to override our natural selfish instincts and give agape in order to be friends. Most of us just cannot do this by ourselves. Our flesh gets in the way. How can we give to someone who makes us feel unsafe? How can we give to our enemies? This concept of giving agape to establish philia is just too much for mere mortals to comprehend. What could possibly motivate us to give this soul-healing love to our perceived enemy? The answer is simple but not easy: We give unconditional love because we are first loved by God.

In Christ We Are Loved, Lovable, and Loving

Beloved let us love one another, for love is from God and everyone who loves is born of God and knows God. The one who does not love does not know God, for God is love. By this the love of God was manifested in us, that God has sent his only begotten Son into the world so that we might live through Him. This is love, not that we loved God, but that He loved us and sent his Son to be a propitiation for our sins. Beloved if God so loved us, we also ought to love one another (1 Jn 4:7–11).

You shall love your neighbor as yourself (Mt 24:39).

Maybe that is the problem, we love our spouses as we love (or do not love) ourselves. If we do not love ourselves, then how are we going to love our partners? If we do not feel loved or lovable, then how are we going to be loving? We felt the Lord gave us the answer to this question one day as we were spending time with our own children.

We were watching our daughters play, as many doting parents do. We were amazed that God would give us two such wonderful and beautiful gifts. As we stared at them, we began to look for similarities between them and us.

"Amanda has your hands," I said to Tom. "Nicole has your eyes and hair. She looks just like you did in your baby pictures."

"Nicole is the spitting image of you, personality wise," Tom said to me, "She has your smile."

Then it hit us. Our children were created in our image, and we cannot help but love them! Likewise, then, we are created in God's image, and he cannot help but love us! We are lovable, because God loves simple little humans like us. The idea that the Creator of the Universe loves us unconditionally, without our striving to earn it, caused us to choke up right there on the playground. As we softly wept there together, we felt the warmth of God's love all around us. We felt worthy. We felt valuable. We felt lovable. The awesome power of this lovability enables us to love, or agape, each other. Thus we can offer unconditional love to our undeserving partner, because God first gave it to us. This unmerited agape from God fills us up. It is out of this fullness that we can give to our mate.

The Endless Cycle of Giving and Receiving

As God's children, you give because Christ Jesus first gave to you, just like the Scripture says. You do not have to rely on your weak human abilities to heal your marriage. You now have the power of your Lord to help you. It is by the Lord's power that your selfish human nature can extend agape to your partner. As your mate receives your love and feels its undeserved merit and favor, he or she feels propelled to reciprocate by giving agape to you. This creates an endless cycle of giving and receiving.

Tom and I found this to be true in our own marriage. When we first met, Eros was hard at work. We had a great deal of chemistry and attraction nudging us that created a desire in us to give to each other. We wanted to meet each other's needs. We did so spontaneously, without thought of what we were getting out of it for ourselves. When the power struggle hit, we were devastated. Our loving partner and friend, whom we had equated as close to Jesus, had now become Lucifer incarnate! Our good and trusted friend was now our foe! This was particularly difficult for me, because I had grown up in such an abusive home. I was counting on my marriage to be a place of healing for me, not of further abuse. My desire to give withered, as my pain and hurt grew. So did Tom's. We loved each other, but we were becoming distant, untrusting, unsafe, and uncaring. We became intimate enemies. It was God's grace, and our commitment to a Christian marriage that kept us looking for ways to bridge the gap. Even as marriage counselors, we thought all the things that couples think in this despair:

He just doesn't care anymore.

She just wants things her way.

This situation is hopeless! He'll never change.

She's been that way for years, what makes me think she'll be different now?

Maybe I just want too much.

Maybe you just want too much.

Is there something wrong with me?

Is there something wrong with you?

Maybe I just married the wrong person.

Amid all the frustrations of our marital power struggle, I did not stop searching for healing and happiness. At times I wondered about my determined quest for soul-healing oneness. I wondered if I just kept up the search because I am so stubborn by nature. Maybe it was because I had been a marriage counselor for so long, and I had learned to believe in this healing process. Maybe I was just a romantic optimist and liked old movies that ended happily ever after. Actually, my searching was a result of the healing that God had already done in my life.

Here I was, with a childhood history of physical, verbal, mental, and emotional abuse. I remember taking a class on the Abnormal Family in graduate school and finding that I had all twelve dysfunctions in my immediate and extended family. I should have been a candidate for a mental institution, not for matrimonial bliss. But despite all the pain and hurt I had suffered at the hands of my earthly caretakers, I felt God's hand reach out to me and bring supernatural healing to my life. As a pathetic hillbilly child with a negative self-esteem score, and a family with a history of extreme dysfunction, there were many times when I thought life was not worth living. These suicidal urgings are not uncommon for adult children of dysfunction.

These hopeless feelings stayed with me until I became a Christian. Christianity brought healing and hope to my wounded soul. It was this healing that propelled my quest for the healing of the soul of my marriage and other marriages like it. This search led me to the door of the Creator and Originator of marital oneness. I found the solution to my dilemma at the feet of the Great Physician, the Omnipotent Marriage Counselor, the Author and Example of Oneness—Jesus Christ. I realized that Christ had already shown us how to do marriage. His relationship with us is our example of matrimony. He loves us with Eros, not romantic love, but the more rudimentary definition, "life energy." Christ's love for us gives us life breath, or life force. This life force provides us with a clear purpose for our existence. However, our sinful nature causes us to fall short, and we disappoint him. Instead of withdrawing or punishing us, he extends his loving hand of agape to us. His unconditional love for us builds a bond of friendship or philia between Jesus and his children. Being regarded and treated as the Lord's friend heals our souls and moves us toward our original life force or life energy. Thus, we recapture our original Eros, as is shown in the following diagram:

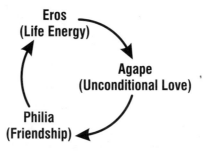

Eros
(Life Energy)

Agape
(Unconditional Love)

Philia
(Friendship)

This is also what God intended for us as married couples. We are attracted to our partners because of our unconscious mating processes and instincts (see Chapter 6). These mating rituals are fueled by our need for life energy or Eros. Finding our life energy motivates us to give to our partner. When times get hard in a marriage (and they will), this life energy or Eros fades from the repeated washings in hurt and pain. This is when agape becomes necessary. It is Jesus, the author of agape, who gives couples the strength they need to love each other unconditionally. From this love, the bond of friendship or philia is built. Couples become friends and commit to healing each other's soul. The energy that comes from this friendship stimulates the soul back toward its authentic wholeness, back to its life force or life energy, back to Eros where it started. As a couple we move from Eros (life energy) to agape (unconditional love) to philia (friendship) and back to our original Eros. Our marital journey follows the path that the Lord has traveled as our example.

Yes, you return to Eros, complete with positive energy, affection, care, and even some romance. You may even recapture some of the original passion and spark that were so much a part of your courtship. Your heart may partially skip a beat when your long-term mate enters the room. You may briefly become weak-kneed when you see your partner in a crowded shopping mall. You might play together and act like kids again. It is possible that you can rediscover why you fell in love in the first place so many years ago.

From reading the previous chapters, you know that phenylethylamine is released when people fall in love. But as you also learned, studies show that the continued presence of a long-term partner gradually steps up the production of endorphins in the brain. Unlike those crazy, hyped "amphetamines," these are soothing chemicals, natural pain killers similar to narcotics. These endorphins give long-term partners a sense of security, peace, and calm. Thus, couples move from early love, fueled by "amphetamines," to mature love that is laced with pleasant, mellow "narcotics" (Toufexis 50–51).

Couples go from loving someone for what he or she can do for them, to loving someone for who he or she really is. They move from selfishness to giving, from narcissism to altruism, from passion to compassion, from falling in love to deciding to love. The result is that you have a partner to accompany you on your journey through life. You have a companion who knows and cares about your soul pain, and you have and have become a soul healer. This, after all, is what marriage is all about.

Epilogue

With bells ringing and happiness of heart
Our new life together was about to start
It was all so new, an exciting dream
But with all the changes, it never seemed—
We would learn to love each other as we should

Being married wasn't easy, so many people said
A lot of people quit, but we worked at it instead
We hardly made it through those difficult beginning years
Our only consolation was that the Lord knew all our fears
After having it so hard, I recollect in tears—
That maybe now, we can learn to love as we should

We could hardly wait for our baby to arrive
It seemed so hard to see that our love was now alive
She brought us so much joy and happiness to share
I can't tell you what it meant to me, just having you there
Maybe now we can dare—
To love each other as we should

With the busy life of diapers, and all the care a baby takes
Sometimes our "couple time" was difficult to make
The laundry, the bottles, the four a.m. feedings
And many times our eyes were so desperately pleading—
For us to love each other as we should

But there was tap and ballet
And another child on the way
And gradually more and more duties filled our day
So sometimes we ignored what each other had to say
And that made it even harder—
To love each other as we should

We sat with each other through fevers and such
I never really told you I appreciated it so much
Your support meant so much to me, I often used it as
*   a crutch*
If only we had time to allow our hearts to touch—
Then maybe we could learn to love each other as we should

It seems like only yesterday, our precious gems were small
I can't believe they're married and they don't even call
But the quietness in our home is the worst pain of all—
Maybe now we can learn to love each other as we should

But your job went sour and that caused you so much pain
You gave so much to them, and there was nothing you
*   could gain*
I felt so useless in helping you
I thought you'd never be the same—
Now I know we need to learn to love each other as
*   we should*

Growing older isn't easy. No one warned us of the woes
The moans, the aches, the groans, the sags,
Always keep us on or off our toes
"We're not getting any younger,"
Isn't that how the old song goes
Now maybe we will have the time—
To love each other as we should

I can't believe it's you, lying there in that hospital bed
After all the things we vowed, after all the things we said
I was just learning to love you
And now they say you're dead—
Oh God! Why didn't we learn to love each other as
    we should

If I had to do it over, I'd love you more in every way
I'd give to you, not think of me, and put my concerns away
But a lonely tombstone has nothing left to say
So I come here tearfully each and every day—
Praying to the Lord that you will forgive me
For never taking the time to learn to love you as I should[1]

The journey to becoming a soul healer is an exciting one; please don't wait. May God richly bless you, as you embark.

Notes

Chapter 2

1. *Webster's College Dictionary* (New York: Random House,1995), s.v. "soul."
2. *Grolier's Encyclopedia on CD-ROM* (Electronic Publishing, 1993), s.v. "soul."

Chapter 3

1. From a discussion at a Training Session for Certified Imago Relationship Therapists.

Chapter 4

1. From an Imago Therapy Training session for therapists.

Chapter 8

1. *Webster's* (New York: Random House, 1995), s.v. "projection."
2. James Strong, *Strong's Exhaustive Concordance of the Bible with Greek and Hebrew Dictionary*, (Gordonville, Tenn.: Dungan Publishers, n.d.), s.v. "way" or "derek."

Chapter 10

1. From an Imago Therapy Training session for therapists.
2. From *Healing the Shame that Binds You*. See also *Creating Love*.
3. *Mirroring* is a term used in Imago Therapy, *active listening* is used in Parent Effectiveness Training, and *parroting* is used in some of Gary Smalley's communication training.

Epilogue

1. Written by Beverly after the birth of our second child, Nicole Renaé Rodgers, December 20,1983.

Bibliography

Bass, Allison. "What Makes Marriages Fail." *The Charlotte Observer* 12 (Dec. 1993): E-1–3.

Beattie, Melody. *Beyond Codependency*. New York: Harper and Row, 1989.

Boze-MeniNage, Ivan, and Geraldine Sparks. *Invisible Loyalties*. New York: Brunner/Mazel,1983.

Bradshaw, John. *Creating Love*. New York: Bantam,1992.

———. *Healing the Shame That Binds You*. Deerfield Beach, Fla.: Health Communications, 1988.

Brand, Paul. "The Gift of Pain." *Christianity Today* 38, no. 1 (10 Jan. 1994): 18–24.

Crabb, Larry. *The Marriage Builder*. Grand Rapids: Zondervan, 1992.

Farmer, Steven. *Adult Children of Abusive Parents: A Healing Program for Those Who Have Been Physically, Sexually, or Emotionally Abused*. New York: Ballantine Books, 1989.

Fisher, Helen. *The Anatomy of Love: The Natural History of Monogamy, Adultery, and Divorce*. New York: Norton, 1992.

Forward, Susan, and Joan Torres. *Toxic Parents*. New York: Bantam,1987.

Freud, Sigmund. *Collected Papers 4*. New York: Basic Books, 1959.

Gray, Paul. "What Is Love." *Time* 104, no. 6 (15 Feb. 1993): 47–48.

Harlow, Harry. *Learning to Love*. New York: Jason Aronson,1974.

Hemfelt, Robert; Frank Minirth; and Paul Meier. *Love Is a Choice*. Nashville: Thomas Nelson, 1989.

Hendrix, Harville. *Getting the Love You Want*. New York: Harper Perennial, 1990.

———. *Keeping the Love You Find*. New York: Pocket Books, 1992.

Lauer, Jeanette and Robert Lauer. "Marriages Made to Last." *Psychology Today* 19, no 6 (June 1985): 85–89.

Love, Patricia. *The Emotional Incest Syndrome: When a Parent's Love Rules Your Life*. New York: Bantam,1990.

Moore, Thomas. *Soul Mates*. New York: Harper Perennial, 1992.

———. *The Care of the Soul*. New York: Harper Perennial, 1994.

Ornstein, Robert, and David Sobel. *The Healing Brain*. New York: Simon and Schuster, 1987.

Robinson, Bryan. *Heal Your Self-Esteem*. Deerfield Beach, Fla.: Health Communications, 1991.

———. *Overdoing It*. Deerfield Beach, Fla.: Health Communications, 1994.

Sanford, John. *The Invisible Partners*. New York: Paulist Press, 1980.

Sanford, John, and Paula Sanford. *The Transformation of the Inner Man*. New York: Bridge Publishers, 1982.

Seamands, David. *Healing Damaged Emotions*. Wheaton, Ill.: Victor Books,1981.

———. *Healing Grace*. Wheaton, Ill.: Victor Books, 1988.

Smalley, Gary. *Making Love Last Forever*. Dallas: Word, 1996.

Smalley, Gary, and John Trent. *Love Is a Decision*. New York: Inspirational Press, 1989.

Smedes, Lewis. *Forgive and Forget: Healing the Hurts You Don't Deserve. .* San Francisco: Harper and Row, 1984.

Springle, Pat. *Close Enough to Care*. Dallas: Rapha/Word, 1990.

Stuart, Richard. *Helping Couples Change: A Social Learning Approach to Marital Therapy*. New York: Guilford Press, 1980.

Tennov, Dorothy. *Love and Limmerence*. New York: Stein & Day, 1970.

Toufexis, Anastasia. "The Right Chemistry." *Time* 104, no. 6 (5 Feb. 1993): 49–51.

Vine, W. E. *Vine's Expository Dictionary of New Testament Words*. McLean, Va.: MacDonald Publishing Co., 1990.

W., Bill. *Alcoholics Anonymous Comes of Age: A Brief History of AA*. Alcoholics Anonymous World Services, 1957, 1975.

Waitley, Denis. *Seeds of Greatness*. Old Tappan, N.J.: Fleming Revell, 1983.

Warren, Neal. *Finding the Love of Your Life: Ten Principles to Choosing the Right Marriage Partner*. New York: Pocket Books, 1992.

Woititz, Janet. *Adult Children of Alcoholics*. Deerfield Beach, Fla.: Health Communications, 1983.

———. *Struggle for Intimacy*. Deerfield Beach, Fla.: Health Communications, 1985.

Resources For Parenting

AT-HOME MOTHERHOOD
Making It Work for You

Cindy Tolliver

Paper, 152 pages, 6" x 9"
ISBN:0-89390-295-0

This book validates your choice as an at-home mother and guides you toward exploring relationships, handling practical matters, and doing self-development. Read this book and feel comfortable about your choices.

VELVET AND STEEL
A Practical Guide for Christian Fathers and Grandfathers

John K. Ream

Paper, 160 pages, 6" x 9"
ISBN:0-89390-408-2

Ream explains what it means to be a man in this day and age and how men can strengthen their families by compassion (velvet) with moral backbone (steel). He tells men how to get back in the game, how to assess their current family situation, how to begin a prayer partnership with their wives, and how to step through the land mines of fatherhood, from raising babies to enjoying grandchildren. With this book, men can discover how putting their faith first can pay great dividends for themselves and their families.

WHAT TO DO WHEN YOUR KIDS TALK DIRTY

Timothy Jay, PhD

Perfectbound, 160 pages, 5.5" x 8.5"
ISBN:0-89390-412-0

Timothy Jay, author of *What to Do When Your Students Talk Dirty,* has followed up with this companion book for parents. Jay shows parents how to clarify which language values are important to them. Then he shows them how to use proven management techniques to improve the quality of their children's language. Useful for parents of children of any age, including teenagers.

See the last page for ordering information.

Resources for Facing Crises

OUR FAMILY IS DIVORCING
A Read-Aloud Book for Families Experiencing Divorce
Patricia Polin Johnson and Donna Reilly Williams

Paper, 64 pages, 6" x 9", illustrated,
ISBN:0-89390-391-4

If you work with children of divorcing parents, *Our Family Is Divorcing* should be on your bookshelf. For referral to parents. For group work with children who hurt. For reading aloud to the individual child. This illustrated book tells the story of Mandy, Spencer, and Eddie whose parents are divorcing. A special section tells caregivers how to use the book to help children to understand their feelings about their parents' divorce and to cope with a changing family system.

WHEN YOUR LONG-TERM MARRIAGE ENDS
A Workbook for Divorced Women
Elaine Newell

Paper, 144 pages, 6" x 9"
ISBN:0-89390-291-8

When Your Long-Term Marriage Ends is a workbook written especially for the woman who finds herself facing the challenging transition of a divorce. This book leads the reader through the stages of panic, rejection, anger, loneliness, awareness, responsibility, and, finally, forgiveness.

WHEN YOU ARE THE PARTNER OF A RAPE OR INCEST SURVIVOR
A Workbook for You
Robert Barry Levine

Paper, 104 pages, 6" x 9"
ISBN:0-89390-329-9

The partners of rape or incest victims are also victims. As a partner of a rape-or incest-survivor, you may feel that you, too, must keep your pain, suffering and anger a secret. This workbook benefits survivors because its approach is sensitive to many of the key issues survivors face in their healing process. It also teaches you, the partner, how to be supportive to the survivor's needs, while becoming aware of and dealing with your own needs and concerns.

See the last page for ordering information.

Resources For Personal Growth

HOW TO FIND MR. OR MS. RIGHT
A Practical Guide to Finding a Soul Mate

Beverly and Tom Rodgers

Paper, 160 pages, 6 x 9
ISBN: 0-89390-451-1

Here's a practical guide with easy-to-do exercises including "Your Soul Mate Profile" tool to help evaluate prospective partners. Learn how to stop picking the wrong kind of people and stop running off the right kind of people.

BALANCING YOUR LIFE
Setting Personal Goals

Paul Stevens

Paper, 96 pages, 4.25" x 7"
ISBN:0-89390-375-2

The key to improving your life, according to noted worklife expert Paul Stevens, is planning. *Balancing Your Life: Setting Personal Goals* will help you sort through the conflicting issues you deal with each day, the opportunities you want to explore, and the actions you need to take to bring balance to your life. In the end, you'll emerge with a set of clear personal goals that will put you in charge of your dreams.

MEN ARE NO DAMN GOOD
(Pending Further Research) Essays on Becoming a Man
Eugene J. Webb; Illustrator: C.P. Houston

Paper, 192 pages, 5.5" x 8.5"
ISBN:0-89390-343-4

How do you get men to talk about their stuff? With a light touch. Webb's wry wit eases men into the deep issues and invites them to ponder: their heroes, finding purpose, facing embarrassment, facing fatherhood, sexual uncertainty, belonging, leaving, and death. Each essay is preceded by a forethought and followed by an afterthought with questions to help you reflect on the deep themes raised. Who knows? You may find that men are okay after all.

Order from your local bookseller, or contact:

 Resource Publications, Inc.
160 E. Virginia Street #290
San Jose, CA 95112-5876
1-408-286-8505 (questions), 1-888-273-7782 (orders, toll-free)
1-408-287-8748 (fax)
info@rpinet.com
www.rpinet.com   SH